Personnel Policies, Training & Development

Hodder & Stoughton

A MEMBER OF THE HODDER HEADLINE GROUP

Orders; please contact Bookpoint Ltd, 78 Milton Park, Abingdon, Oxon OX14 4TD. Telephone: (44) 01235 400414, Fax: (44) 01235 400454. Lines are open from 9.00–6.00, Monday to Saturday, with a 24 hour message answering service.
Email address: orders@bookpoint.co.uk

British Library Cataloguing in Publication Data
A catalogue record for this title is available from the British Library

ISBN 0 340 74289 5

First published 1999

Impression number	10 9 8 7 6 5 4 3 2 1
Year	2005 2004 2003 2002 2001 2000 1999

Typeset by GreenGate Publishing Services, Tonbridge, Kent.
Printed in Great Britain for Hodder and Stoughton Educational, a division of Hodder Headline Plc, 338 Euston Road, London NW1 3BH, by Redwood Books, Trowbridge, Wiltshire

Contents

the Institute of Management

FOUNDATION

The mission of the Institute of Management (IM) is to promote the art and science of management.

The Instititue embraces all levels of management from student to chief executive and supports its own Foundation which provides a unique portfolio of services for all managers, enabling them to develop skills and achieve management excellence.

For information on the various levels and benefits of membership, please contact:

Department HS
Institute of Management
Cottingham Road
Corby
Northants NN17 1TT
Tel: 01536 204222
Fax: 01536 201651

Preface

The first Business Checklists were launched by the Institute of Management in 1995. They met with immediate success from managers in all sectors of commerce and industry, and in organisations of all shapes and sizes.

They originated from one simple idea – that managers did not have the time, or indeed the inclination, to plough through heavy tomes of turgid prose in order to unearth the odd nugget or two which might enable them to do their jobs a little better. They also drew their origins from a former series of Checklists by the British Institute of Management which had been successful in the 1970s.

So why are they so successful? Basically because they cut out unnecessary waffle. They express in clear, concise language what managers need to know, and are presented in a consistent format so that it is easy to pick out the bits you want. They have a wide application, outside business as well as inside, and in small or large organisations: introducing a concept or technique, explaining the pros and cons, dos and don'ts, and steps to follow to get you started. They also provide further pointers for those who do have the time, inclination or need to pursue the topic in greater depth.

Updated and revised since their launch, the Business Checklists are here presented for the first time in a series of books which bring them together under broad management functions.

How are the subjects chosen? Not by guesswork or experts who think they know best, but by demand. The Institute's Management Information Centre handles over 50,000 enquiries a year so the Centre's researchers not only have a good idea of what managers are looking for but also how they want it delivered.

Each checklist follows a similar pattern:

MCI Standards

The MCI Management Standards are the underpinning structure for many vocational management qualifications. Each checklist identifies the appropriate subject content of the standards that it meets.

Definition

Clarifies the coverage of the checklist, highlighting both what is and what is not included in its scope.

Advantages and disadvantages

Each checklist highlights the benefits and pitfalls of the topic, providing a quick insight into the experiences of others.

Action checklist

The core of the checklist is the step-by-step sequence, written in jargon-free language and designed to help readers get to grips with a task quickly.

Dos and don'ts

A brief summary of the key items to remember – and to avoid – on each topic.

Useful reading and organisations

Sources of additional information for readers wishing to investigate the topic further.

Thought starters

Some introductory ideas to help readers begin to approach the subject in a practical way.

Although the Business Checklists constitute a wide-ranging, but concise, library of management know-how, we don't pretend – yet – that they are complete. As they are being continually updated and revised, please get in touch with the Institute of Management's Information Centre in Corby if you have suggestions for future editions.

Bob Norton
Head of Information Services
Institute of Management.

Planning the Recruitment Process

This checklist deals with the recruitment process from the moment the current postholder resigns or when a need for another person is perceived, through to the drawing up of a short-list from which to interview.

Recruitment is an expensive process in its own right, but it can also have costly implications if the appropriate people are not identified, both in terms of the performance of the organisation and high labour turnover. To minimise these problems, a planned approach to recruitment allows a systematic review of the organisation's employment needs and the way to achieve them.

MCI Standards

This checklist has relevance for the MCI Management Standards: Key Role C – Manage People.

Definition

The first half of the recruitment process, before conducting interviews, is concerned with verifying that you have a vacancy, identifying the sort of person you are looking for and in what capacity, finding them and making a short-list.

Advantages of planned recruitment

It:

- allows you to ensure that you really have a post to fill
- offers you the opportunity to re-evaluate the existing position to see if a different type of job specification is needed
- lets you decide on what basis you wish to employ somebody
- ensures that you consider all possible avenues for finding the person.

Disadvantages

- Time consuming.
- May lead to delays in making an appointment.

Action checklist

1. Decide if you have a vacancy

Review whether you have a need for the work to be carried out at all or whether it can be incorporated into somebody else's job. If you have a vacancy assess whether you need a full-time, permanent member of staff. Would a temporary or part-time employee be sufficient? Consider the use of an agency or consultancy to supply staff on the basis you want, or outsourcing the work altogether.

2. Consult other staff who are involved

You will probably need to get authorisation to appoint or re-appoint from senior management. Consider other departments in the organisation which might be interested in the appointment; you might want to make it a joint effort. Talk to the previous holder of the post where possible, to the relevant supervisor and especially to the people the new person will work with. Consult the personnel department, if you have one, because they will be able to lend you their expertise. Decide who is to interview applicants as they may want some say at an early stage.

3. Work out the sort of person you are looking for

List the duties, responsibilities, authority and relationships which the job involves. If you are filling a post that is being vacated, assess whether you want it carried out in the same way as before or whether there are changes that you wish to make. Decide what qualifications are needed, what type and length of experience are required, and what personal attributes are important. On this basis you can then draw up an up-to-date job description and person specification. Forecast how soon the person is expected to be competent, what training you are prepared to give and when the start date of the job should be.

4. Find out if they exist

Ask yourself whether you are likely to find the qualities, qualifications and experience that you are seeking in one person. If so, research the kind of pay and benefits package you will have to offer. This can be done through monitoring local and national advertisements, referring to salary surveys (often expensive but usually summarised in the press at time of publication) and networking with other employers in your area and sector. This research will also give you a feel for whether you are likely to find suitable candidates locally or whether you will have to look further afield. Start thinking about whether people will want to join your organisation and about how to attract them.

5. Plan how you will find them

Start within your own organisation. Are there suitable employees ready for this opportunity? Even if your assessment is negative, ensure that you advertise the post internally, both as a courtesy to staff and because they may pass the information on to any interested friends and relations. Word of mouth can be a valuable recruitment method, but guard against the gender and racial imbalances that this practice may perpetuate. Check previous applications, whether unsolicited or not. Draw on any appropriate contacts you have, for example relevant training schools, useful whether you are looking for apprentices or MBAs. Decide at this point whether to use the services of a recruitment agency to find and short-list applicants for you. Your decision will be based on the time and expertise you have available and the costs incurred by employing an agency.

6. Decide where to advertise

If you are going it alone, and you need to advertise, pinpoint the part of the press you need to contact. Do you want to use local or national newspapers? If the post is of a specialist nature you may wish to advertise in the journals of professional bodies or the trade press. Find out how much adverts cost for varying amounts of space and decide what you can afford. Consider using local job centres as well as new media such as the Internet, which now has various job pages and mailing lists.

7. Write the advertisement

Decide if you and/or other staff are skilled enough to draw up an advert. If your organisation has a personnel department they will probably take on this task, but do ensure that you are involved throughout the process. In the case of a senior post or if you are recruiting in large numbers, you may feel it appropriate to hire an advertising agency to draft the advert and select where it should appear. It is better to name your organisation in the advert rather than use a box number unless you have particular reasons for secrecy, as a box number could deter some applicants. Ensure that the advert states the following clearly but succinctly:

- the duties and responsibilities of the job
- the qualification and experience required
- the personal qualities sought
- where the job is based

- indications of the salary or type of salary
- what form of reply is demanded (CV or request for an application form)
- whether further information is available and in what form.

Ensure that the advert presents a picture of an interesting and dynamic organisation because many people will notice it, including those who do not apply for the job. More importantly, check that the advert does not contravene any legislation and codes of practice, for example in the areas of sex and racial discrimination. If you intend to ask applicants to use an application form, make sure this form requests all the details you need to assess the candidates. Complete the application form yourself, or get a colleague to do it, from the point of view of applicants, and check its suitability. Prepare an information pack for those who ask.

8. Draw up a short-list

Decide on the length of the short-list, probably five or six people at most. Following your advert you will need help to sift through the applications. It may be outside assistance from an agency of some kind which can use computers if there are large numbers of replies, or from other staff, supervisors or managers in your organisation. Apart from the question of time, it is advisable to get other opinions. Things to look out for when reading an application include how well-matched is the candidate to your requirements, any unexplained employment gaps, the quality of presentation and how tailored the reply is to your particular job and organisation.

9. Reply to candidates

Those whom you have no intention of interviewing should be contacted as quickly as possible and dealt with courteously: they, and their relatives and friends, may be future customers or acquaintances of potential, future applicants. Those whom you do wish to interview should also be contacted as quickly as possible to check that they are still interested in the job and if so to arrange a date and time. Make sure they know where to find you and whether you are willing to meet their expenses. You may wish to keep a small number of candidates in reserve.

Dos and don'ts for advertising a vacancy

Do

- Take the opportunity to review if there is a job to be filled.
- Have a clear idea of who you are looking for.
- Use assistance from at least one other person.
- Assess the market before advertising.

Don't

- Forget the recruitment process has public relations implications.
- Lay your organisation open to charges of discrimination.

Useful reading

Recruitment and selection, Gareth Roberts, London: Institute of Personnel and Development, 1997
Recruitment key facts, London: Institute of Personnel and Development, 1997
Successful recruitment and selection: a practical guide for managers, Margaret Dale, London: Kogan Page, 1997
Fair recruitment and selection, Gerard Lemos, London: Lemos Associates, 1994
How to write a job description, Bernard Ungerson, London: Institute of Personnel Management, 1983

Useful addresses

Industrial Society, Robert Hyde House, 48 Bryanston Square, London W1H 7LN, Tel: 0171 262 2401
Institute of Management, Management House, Cottingham Road, Corby, Northants NN17 1TT, Tel: 01536 204222
Institute of Personnel and Development, 35 Camp Road, London SW19 4UX, Tel: 0181 971 9000

Thought starters

- Is there a high turnover of staff in your organisation?
- What led to past recruitment mistakes?
- What is your own experience of being a candidate in the recruitment process?

Preparing and Using Job Descriptions

This checklist provides guidance for those wishing to write a job description for a new post or to update an existing one.

Drawing up job descriptions for a department helps to ensure that work is organised into jobs that occupy a person full time, and to check that each job is justified. Job descriptions provide the basis for the preparation of key results and objectives for the organisation, each function and each person in it, making sure that these fit into a coherent whole. A job description can help a candidate to gain a picture of what the job is about, and can provide the recruiter with a checklist of requirements against which to match candidates. Once in post, an employee will have a list of main responsibilities and important contacts through direct working relationships. The organisation will find job descriptions essential in job evaluation and assessments; they are also helpful when settling disputes about duties, whilst permitting some flexibility.

MCI Standards

This checklist has relevance for the MCI Management Standards: Key Role C – Manage People.

Definition

A job description is a structured and factual statement of a job's function and objectives, the acceptable standards of performance and the boundaries of the job holder's authority. The job title, department, location, and to and for whom the job holder is responsible, are also included.

Advantages of job descriptions

Job descriptions:

- are useful in the recruitment process
- are an aid in planning objectives and obtaining training requirements
- are essential for clarifying boundaries of responsibility and decision making.

Disadvantages of job descriptions

They:

- can create a 'that's not in my job description!' environment if too restrictive
- need regular updating.

Action checklist

1. Inform staff of the reasons for reviewing and amending job descriptions

When existing job descriptions are reviewed, it is important to inform employees what is happening and why, to guard against employees feeling threatened. A statement should be made to the effect that the exercise will be carried out, with the full involvement of the job holders, with the objectives being, for example:

- to identify all interdepartmental working links
- to help plan objectives and training programmes
- to ensure that functions have the correct number of staff for their workload
- to give everyone a clear understanding of how the company is organised.

2. Assign responsibility

In some cases job descriptions are prepared by personnel departments and agreed with the job holder and manager, but this is generally undesirable. The exercise should be done by the job holder and manager with guidance about form and content available from the personnel department.

A central function, usually the personnel department, should be assigned to check job descriptions for consistency and overlap. In doing this the following points should be considered:

- Does each job holder have a clear line of authority?
- Does each job holder report to the right person?
- Do too many employees report directly to one manager, who may be unable to cope with their supervision properly?
- Are there too many levels of authority?
- Are some jobs so similar as to be essentially the same?
- Are staff and line functions clearly defined?
- Are similar functions grouped together or are there odd jobs in unrelated departments which clearly belong elsewhere?
- Are specific tasks and objectives passed down from the centre which can be followed downwards through individual job descriptions?

- Are there any 'gaps', ie jobs for which no one has been assigned responsibility?

3. Gather information

The person responsible for compiling the job description should consider:

- what management wants from the job
- what the job holder thinks he or she is doing and what he or she is actually doing
- what others, whose work interacts with the job holder, think he or she is doing and ought to be doing.

This information should be gained from informal interviews. If resources are limited, it is possible to use questionnaires, but the results tend to be ambiguous, and the time required to analyse the completed questionnaires can exceed the interviewing time. Employees can be asked to complete a diary over a short period of time, but generally employees dislike this, and it should be avoided.

4. Put together the job description

The job description should contain:

a) Basic information

Job title and department – the job title should be readily understood inside and outside the organisation. Remember that other employees will consider the status of those with the same kind of job title to be equal. Do not use over-elaborate job titles.

Location – the location of the job should be given. If some flexibility is expected then it is wise not to define the location too tightly, but to state that the normal location may change from time to time.

Responsibility to – the names of the people who are responsible for supervision, discipline, etc.

Responsibility for – include the total number of staff for whom they are responsible, with the names of those reporting directly to the job holder. For example, 'responsible for 30 staff through three supervisors'.

Major functional relationships – an organisation chart will show how a job fits into the organisation and its relationship with other jobs. For example, a works personnel officer may report directly to the works manager but a dotted line should also show the personnel officer reporting to the company personnel manager.

b) Principal purpose or objective of the job
This should be a short statement describing why the job exists. For example, for a sales manager it could be simply 'ensuring that sales targets are achieved'.

c) Main duties/key tasks/key result areas
Key tasks, or responsibilities, are those which make a substantial contribution towards the job objectives and those of the organisation. These form the main part of the job description and there should be no more than eight to ten tasks listed, rather than a list of all the job holder's tasks. To ensure against too restrictive a job description, an open-ended statement should be included. A standard statement is: 'Such duties as are considered essential for effective operations and services'. This should form the final key task. Distinguish between those tasks which are the direct responsibility of the job holder and those which he or she delegates to others to carry out.

The job description should allow for an individual to use his or her initiative, and where results are measurable in some way the measures should be stated. Results expected should be concrete, specific, attainable and worthwhile. Where levels of achievement are specified in measurements, it is particularly important that these are regularly updated.

Once the key tasks have been identified they should be put into some sort of order, which might be chronological, by relative importance, by frequency of performance, by similar sorts of tasks, or by all tasks related to a particular aspect of the job. Each task should be described in a sentence or two which explains what is done, how and why. Sentences should begin with action verbs, with imprecise phrases like 'responsible for' avoided.

5. Update and review

The job description must be kept up-to-date and should be examined at least:

- once a year when the job holder is appraised
- when a job falls vacant, to ensure that the description still meets the department's requirements
- after the new job holder has been in post a few months to take account of any significant changes in the job holder's duties.

Dos and don'ts for preparing a job description

Do
- Involve the current job holder.
- Check job descriptions in 'surrounding' areas of work to ensure a close fit and no clashes.
- Make updating job descriptions a regular process.

Don't

- Forget to let staff know why job descriptions are being amended or updated.
- Restrict the employee's initiative through the job description.

Useful reading

Books

How to write a job description, Bernard Ungerson, London: Institute of Personnel Management, 1983

A guide to writing job descriptions, International Computers Limited Remuneration Planning Department, London: International Computers Limited, nd

Journal articles

The importance of the job description, Frank Walton, Employment Bulletin and Industrial Relations Digest, Vol 5 no 2, February 1989, pp5–7

Writing job descriptions that get results, Roger J Plachy, Personnel, October 1987, pp56–63

Thought starters

- Do you know what's in your job description?
- Would you change your job description in any way?
- Is your job description up-to-date?

Steps in Successful Selection Interviewing

This checklist is designed to help managers conduct successful selection interviews.

The job interview is still the most widely used recruitment tool, in spite of the increasing interest in other techniques such as the use of biodata, graphology, personality tests or assessment centres. There are three principal interview models:

- **the biographical interview – exploring the candidate's experiences**
- **the behavioural interview – eliciting information about how applicants have behaved in similar situations**
- **the situational interview – comprising a series of job-related questions.**

Many interviewers (or organisations) prefer to use one technique, but these different models can be useful in different situations. This checklist helps interviewers plan, prepare and conduct interviews, regardless of the interview approach they adopt.

MCI Standards

This checklist has relevance for the MCI Management Standards: Key Role C – Manage People.

Definition

Recruitment and selection interviews assess (or partly assess, in conjunction with other methods) an individual's suitability for a job either inside or outside their current organisation.

Advantages of selection interviews

- Selecting new employees by means of a well-designed process can avoid bad recruitment, which is costly to the organisation.
- Information in addition to that supplied by candidates in their application can be gained or verified.
- Candidates can learn more about the organisation than would otherwise be possible.

Drawbacks of selection interviews

There is some doubt that an interview is the most appropriate mechanism for assessing candidates' suitability with accuracy, witness:

- First impressions are often lasting impressions; decisions tend to be made early on in the interview.
- Interviewers may prefer candidates who are like themselves, which may lead to discrimination.
- There is a danger of being selective – only hearing information which supports preconceptions or first impressions.
- Interviewers can get jaded and confused if too many interviews are held in one day – early interviews get forgotten and later ones are less effective.

Action checklist

1. Narrow the search

Interviewing is a fairly late step in the recruitment process, and follows the drawing up of a job description and person specification, placing advertisements and shortlisting candidates. (These points are covered in Planning the Recruitment Process, Using Psychometric Tests and Preparing and Using Job Descriptions). The information collected from these processes will form the basis of the criteria against which candidates may be judged.

2. Prepare yourself for the interview

To obtain maximum benefit from the interviewing process, careful planning and preparation are essential. Some organisations have particular styles of interview that they prefer. Check the policies of your own organisation and ensure you adhere to them, following all the necessary practices and completing required paperwork.

- **Style** – Interviews can take many forms – one to one, sequential one to one, panel interviews – which can be complemented by tests, presentations, group discussions and social events. Once the format has been decided, it is always advisable to brief all the people involved, including reception staff, and staff in the department of the vacancy. If several people are involved in interviewing, a chairman should be appointed. Decide how long each will hold the stage and what sort of questions will be asked.

- **Schedule** – Scheduling the day(s) realistically is crucial. Always running behind and keeping interviewees waiting for extended periods can give a bad impression of the organisation. Draw up a schedule which allows time to interview, reflect, write notes and prepare for the next person. Plan too for some breaks, as interviewing can prove gruelling.

- **Documentation** – The application form or CV, person specification and job description are essential documents to have before you. Read through all the relevant material beforehand, noting or highlighting particular areas of interest.
- **Environment** – Think carefully about the environment you want to create. Your choice of room, chairs and layout is important to the interview. No distractions of any kind are to be permitted: they disrupt the natural flow of the interview and can disturb the candidate. Put a notice on the door, divert phone calls or take the phone off the hook. If interruptions are still possible, identify and book another location.

3. Inform candidates that they have been selected for interview

Inform candidates in writing that they have been selected for interview, and of the date and time of their interview. This should be done with a reasonable notice period (a week may be sufficient, but with more senior posts longer notice is desirable). Decide what you will do if the candidate genuinely cannot come on the specified date. Include in the information sent:

- a location map and details of public transport
- details of the length of time the candidate will be involved with the interview
- the format of the interview (whether the candidate will be expected to take a psychometric test, for example).

4. Work out how to record how each candidate performs

You may decide to develop a scoring or recording method, particularly if more than one person is involved in the interview process or if more than three or four interviews are to be held. This can bring some method to establishing, remembering and measuring the key points which can affect decision making. Weight the criteria you have established for the post and be prepared to assign points against these for each candidate as the interview progresses.

5. Plan the questions to ask

Questions can take many forms – open, hypothetical, leading, probing or closed.

- **Open questions** provide an open platform for the interviewee to structure and steer the response.
- **Hypothetical questions** allow the interviewer to establish how the candidate would act in a certain situation.
- **Leading questions** can tend to make assumptions that the interviewee will confirm or deny.

- **Probing questions** enable the interviewer to probe an issue more fully and can help draw out the whole picture.
- **Closed questions** are useful to establish precise facts, but tend to lead to very short answers (often yes or no).

Beware, however, of discriminatory questions. To comply with the best equal opportunities practice, the same questions should be asked, by the same people, in the same order. This overcomes the problem of asking questions only of specific groups.

6. Prepare for the interviewee's questions

Most interviewees should have some questions which may be asked throughout the interview. It is good practice to check, as the interview closes, if there is anything further they would like to ask or add.

7. Set the stage

At the start of the interview it is essential to put the candidate at their ease. If there are several interviewers, the Chair should introduce them all. Smile, shake their hand and ask light, background questions to establish rapport and create the right climate. At this point in the interview, the planned process should be explained to the candidate and further information about the role and responsibilities should be given.

8. Observe closely, taking body language into account

The key to successful interviewing is to listen carefully and to look deeper than the words expressed. Don't spend time thinking about how to phrase your next question (you should have decided this beforehand): while you are doing so you are not paying full attention to the candidate. Some of the following may give you an indication that perhaps something is not quite right:

- blushing
- nervous hand movements
- sudden loss of eye contact
- twitching, stammering, frowning
- any significant change in the pace of speech
- inconsistency between words and non-verbal messages.

If you notice any of these signs, it may be worth probing more deeply into what the candidate has said. On the other hand it may be explained away as nervousness; the interviewer may then decide to try to help put the interviewee at ease. Watch your own body language too: make it clear to the candidates that they have your continuous full attention.

9. Close the interview constructively

The ending of an interview can be as important as the beginning. It is important to keep to your schedule by not allowing the interview to continue indefinitely. Thank the candidate for attending and explain what will happen next – a final decision or further short-listing. Give an indication of the timescale you intend to work to – ensure you stick to it.

10. Decide on the successful candidate

How you come to a decision can be the most difficult part of the process, particularly if interviewers disagree. Refer back to the scoring method you chose, ensuring you are basing decisions on facts rather than feelings.

11. Practise your interviewing technique

To ensure you succeed in the role of interviewer, it is essential to practise the necessary techniques. Test out your technique on an experienced colleague, and if you are interviewing as a member of a panel, learn from the others and ask for feedback. After each interview, review your performance and look at what you could do differently.

Dos and don'ts for successful selection interviewing

Do

- Prepare thoroughly (including the environment, yourself, questions and other interviewers).
- Check the organisation's policies.
- Watch for inconsistencies between verbal and non-verbal behaviour.

Don't

- Make decisions based on a gut reaction.
- Break your schedule.
- Allow interruptions.
- Talk too much.

Useful reading

Structured employment interviewing, Paul J Taylor and Michael P O'Driscoll, Aldershot: Gower, 1995

Successful interviewing in a week, 2nd ed, Mo Shapiro, London: Hodder & Stoughton, 1998

Sharpen up your interviewing: the systematic approach to effective interviewing for busy managers, Jack Gratus, London: Mercury Books, 1991

Thought starters

- How have those who have interviewed you performed in their role? What would you have done differently?
- What was good/bad about the best/worst interview you've ever had?

Using Psychometric Tests

This checklist is for all who may be considering using psychometric tests in an employment situation; for example, for workshops, counselling, career development, team building, personnel selection or assessment centres.

The administration and interpretation of tests must be carried out by people qualified to an appropriate standard.

MCI Standards

This checklist has relevance for the MCI Management Standards: Key Role C – Manage People.

Definition

A psychometric test is usually but not always in the form of a questionnaire, normally administered on paper, but increasingly by electronic media. There are two main categories of test: **cognitive/mental ability tests**, designed to measure numeracy and verbal skill, and **personality tests**, designed to measure aspects of behaviour. Tests may also be known as 'instruments', 'questionnaires' or 'tools'.

Uses and drawbacks of psychometric tests

Psychometric tests have a strong appeal, by appearing to give precise answers to the complex and intriguing questions about individual personality, and by their implied ability to predict behaviour. This appearance of certainty can, however, be misleading. The reasons for use, method of use and ethical issues involved should always be carefully considered.

Uses of psychometric tests

If used correctly and in the right situation, tests have a number of important applications.

- **Workshops** – Tests may be used as an ingredient in training workshops to improve the efficiency of the learning process. They can provide a vocabulary that can be used in exploring interpersonal reactions, make such exploration more objective, and provide indicators for making behaviour more effective.
- **Counselling** – Tests can help individuals, especially when under pressure or threat (for example, from poor work assessments, dismissal, redundancy, or personality conflict at home or work) to explore their own motivation and behaviour. They are effective as catalysts for open discussion with counsellors or other helpers.
- **Career development or guidance** – Tests can help individuals to identify their strengths and weaknesses, judge how these may impact on their career, and decide on actions to aid their development.
- **Team building** – Tests may help in building teams by providing insight into the team behaviour of individual members, and in indicating aspects in which a team needs additional resources or may benefit from development activities.
- **Personnel selection and assessment centres** – In job selection, tests can be used to generate open and more objective discussion between candidate and selector. They may have the potential to predict likely future behaviour in specified roles or situations, although this function must be treated with caution.

Drawbacks of psychometric tests

- **Expense** – The costs of choosing a test and training (or using trained) staff to administer and evaluate it can be high. It is important to weigh these costs against the additional help the tests may be able to provide.
- **Ethical problems** – Completing tests can be stressful, and testers should beware of abusing the power this may give. Legal challenges to the fairness of tests, particularly on the grounds of sexual, racial and cultural bias, have been mounted, especially in the USA. In particular, the use of tests for selection for redundancy is under serious challenge and is not recommended.
- **Interpretation** – Of the numerous tests available (currently over 5000) many may be unreliable or unvalidated; others may be unsuitable for specific uses. It is possible to misunderstand results and easy to place too much reliance on them. Unbiased, professional advice is essential in test choice. Test administration and interpretation also require skilled and qualified help.

Action checklist

Action is needed in:

- deciding whether psychometric tests are appropriate
- choosing tests
- running the test programme
- using the results.

1. Deciding whether psychometric tests are appropriate

a) Establish and write down precise objectives for the use of tests.
b) Consider how else the objectives could be attained, and what added value tests might contribute.
c) Make a preliminary assessment of the likely costs of a testing programme, including the training of the tester, purchase and evaluation of tests, staff time and overhead costs.
d) Decide whether the proposed application is efficient and cost-effective.

2. Choosing tests

a) Obtain information from potential, reputable test providers. Obtain guidance, if necessary, from qualified psychologists, the British Psychological Society or other experienced bodies or professional practitioners.
b) Make a short-list of possible tests in discussion with test providers and other professionals, bearing clearly in mind the objectives set (Action 1a above), the possibility of designing a battery of two or more tests, and the level of costs attached to each test.
c) Make your final decision – which may be not to use tests.

3. The test programme

a) Embed the chosen test or tests in an appropriate procedure depending on the use to be made of them. This may also involve interviews, practical exercises, analysis of paperwork (such as application forms, CVs, and references).
b) If used as part of a selection process, ensure that job analysis and candidate profiling have been properly completed.
c) Ensure that all concerned in administering tests have been fully trained.
d) Ensure that the procedure devised, and all instructions for test administration, are rigidly followed throughout.
e) Make sure that accommodation is arranged for testing that ensures privacy and freedom from distraction.
f) Explain the reasons for testing, and how the results will be used, in advance to those tested.
g) Ensure strict confidentiality throughout.
h) Arrange for analysis of test results as quickly as possible.

i) Give sensitive, thorough, feedback to those tested – preferably as an integral part of the procedure.

4. Using the results

a) Ensure that those who will use the results fully understand their significance and limitations.
b) Use test results in conjunction with other evidence and data. Do not assume that they are necessarily more valid or authoritative.
c) Destroy all paperwork as soon as it has been used.

Dos and don'ts for the effective use of tests

Do

- Leave test administration and interpretation to people who have been properly trained.
- Complete any short-listed tests yourself.
- Only use tests in conjunction with other appropriate actions (such as structured interviews etc).
- Remember that 'there is more than one way of skinning a cat'; ie people with quite different personalities may succeed in any given job.
- Ensure that every aspect of the use of tests complies with equal opportunities legislation and organisational policies.

Don't

- Use crude, simple tests which claim to do everything – however aggressively sold.
- Automatically accept test results that are contrary to common sense, or that clash with other, well-founded conclusions.
- Blind people (including yourself) with jargon or psychobabble, and remember the dangers of partial knowledge.
- Keep test material and results with other personal files or papers.
- Use tests in redundancy situations.

How to assess test effectiveness

Always ask producers for proof of the validity of their tests and contact organisations who have experience of their tests for their opinions.

Evaluate the relevance of test content to the work concerned. Judge how candidates might react to the questions.

Assess the extent to which a test can predict job suitability or performance standards. Validity can be determined by the correlation between the test scores of current job holders and levels of performance or by studying the performance of employees who have been tested at a later date – this shows the extent to which predictions have been confirmed in practice.

Useful reading

Psychological testing: a managers guide, 3rd ed, John Toplis, Victor Dulewicz and Clive Fletcher, London: Institute of Personnel and Development, 1997
IPD guide on psychological testing, London: Institute of Personnel and Development, 1997
Psychological testing: a practical management guide, Karen Howard and Joan Springall, Hitchin: Technical Communications, 1996
Understanding psychological testing, Charles Jackson, Leicester: BPS Books, 1996
Personnel testing: a managers guide to establishing a quality workforce, John W Jones, London: Kogan Page, 1994
Using psychometrics: a practical guide to testing and assessment, Robert Edenborough, London: Kogan Page, 1994

Useful address

British Psychological Society, 48 Princess Road East, Leicester, LE1 7DR, Tel: 0116 254 9568

Thought starters

- What benefits do you hope to gain from testing?
- How can you choose suitable tests?
- What effect will testing have on candidates? Will they find them acceptable?
- How much will a testing programme cost?

Drawing Up a Contract of Employment

This checklist details the steps involved in drawing up a contract of employment. It is primarily aimed at new contracts, but many points will also be useful to those who have to modify an existing contract. As with any legal document it is essential that advice is sought before a contract is put into effect.

Legislation does not require that an organisation has to have a formal written contract with its employees, but such a contract can prevent disputes over terms and conditions at a later date, whereas oral agreements can often be called into question.

MCI Standards

This checklist has relevance for the MCI Management Standards: Key Role C – Manage People.

Definition

A contract of employment is a legally enforceable agreement, either oral or written, between an employer and employee that defines terms and conditions to which both parties must adhere. Areas covered include job title, remuneration, holidays, sick pay, location, mobility, and the period of employment. Extra clauses can be added which restrain the employee after termination of employment, or make a certain qualification or confidentiality a prerequisite of the job.

Advantages of contracts of employment

Having well-drafted contracts of employment means that:

- employees can be clear about their rights
- costs incurred by disputes over terms and conditions can be avoided
- the employer can justifiably terminate employment if an employee does not meet the contract's requirements.

Disadvantages of contracts of employment

There are no real disadvantages to contracts of employment. Writing one that is water-tight but allows both parties some flexibility is difficult. Contracts require resources to draw up and review, and if they are badly written they can do the organisation more harm than good.

Action checklist

1. Analyse the job to be contracted

Look at the job description if there is one, as this will provide information on what the employee's job entails. Clauses in the contract must allow the employee to carry out their duties without restrictions. The post may require the person to have a professional qualification – would the person be allowed to continue in the role if the awarding body were to withdraw their professional status?

2. Consider future plans and objectives

Would you expect the size of the workforce to be reduced in the future? If so, a permanent contract may not be appropriate. A particular job title may not be suitable if you have to transfer th[illegible]ployee to a different department; a general title, such as 'Admin[illegible] offer more scope for change. If you have plans to open [illegible] the country, you may need to incorporate [illegible]ployees who will have to work there from [illegible] such as mobility, the organisation can ensure th[illegible]future needs and developments.

3. Look back at [illegible]

The organisation may [illegible] with contracts of employment in the past. This could have be[illegible]ture of the work the organisation does, for example, or an em[illegible] could have left taking some customers with them in the process, or have created some intellectual property whose ownership is disputed, or have resisted relocation because a contractual statement was lacking.

4. Gather information and confer with colleagues

Try to obtain some sample contracts of employment used in organisations in the same field, and get hold of literature relating to the current requirements of personnel legislation. Colleagues can offer good advice over what has and has not worked in the past, both in the current organisation and others in which they may have worked. Trade union representatives can point out contentious issues that may arise.

If your organisation has a legal department, consult it. If not, be prepared to go outside; costs incurred here could well save in the long term.

5. Incorporate written particulars

The Employment Protection (Consolidation) Act (EPCA) 1978 and the Trade Union Reform and Employment Rights Act (TURERA) 1993 require that all employees whose employment lasts over a month, irrespective of the number of hours they work, are given a written statement of employment particulars. The Acts do not make it necessary to include these particulars in a contract of employment but it is advisable that they are, so that the employee has one document which contains all matters relating to their relationship with the employer.

The particulars that must be given to the employee are:

- the employer's and employee's names
- the date the employment started and will end (if fixed term), or the period it is expected to last if temporary
- the rate of remuneration or how it is calculated, and when it is paid
- terms and conditions relating to hours of work, holidays, holiday pay, sickness and sick pay, and pensions and pension schemes
- the notice required to be given by both employee and employer to terminate employment
- any collective agreements which affect the terms and conditions of employment, for example, those negotiated by a trade union (even if the employee is not a member)
- the job title
- disciplinary rules (or reference to a set of disciplinary rules), the person to whom an employee can apply and the manner in which the application is to be made if the employee is not satisfied with a decision concerning a matter of discipline. The legislation requires this only for organisations with over 20 employees.
- the name of the person who can be approached and the procedure to follow regarding any grievance related to employment
- details of the place(s) of work
- the length of time and currency in which remuneration will be made if the employee is required to work abroad for a period of more than one month.

These written particulars must be given to employees within two months of commencement of employment.

In cases where another document can be referred to, such as a disciplinary procedure, a staff handbook can be used. This document must be accessible; a copy should be given to the employee as part of their induction.

6. Consider possible extra clauses

There are a number of clauses that may be included in a contract of employment, depending on the nature of the job and the needs of the organisation.

Relocation expenses – it may be appropriate to include a clause which requires an employee to repay any relocation expenses incurred if they leave within a certain period.

Uniform or clothing – where there is a standard dress code or protective clothing is needed, make this clear in the contract. Check on sex discrimination legislation over differences between male and female appearance.

Qualifications – if the jobholder is required to obtain or hold a certain qualification by a certain date (educational or professional), define which one and the consequences of failing to have it. Where the employee is funded to obtain a qualification, they may be required to repay the cost if they terminate their employment within a certain period.

Driving licence – employment may be terminated if the employee loses their licence.

Mobility – where the employee is expected to work at different bases, make it clear.

Travel – for many jobs it is necessary to travel to meet customers or clients, so you may need to include a clause to cover this. Clerical workers are usually only expected to be as mobile as far as is reasonably possible on a daily commuting basis, whereas managers can be expected to travel as far as the business requires.

Probation – if a probationary period is used for new employees then its length should be given, with the ability to terminate the contract at the end or an earlier date, or to extend the length of the probation. Include a statement which says that permanent employment will be confirmed in writing, subject to the probationary period being completed satisfactorily.

Retirement – it should be made clear that the contract is terminated when the employee reaches the organisation's set retirement age.

Restraints – it is possible in some circumstances to restrain the activities of an employee once employment has terminated. Examples include the use of trade secrets that the individual acquired while working for an organisation, or working for another organisation in the same trade and geographical area. Expert advice is essential here as the law is a minefield in this area; the employer must show that the restraining clauses are no more than what is required to protect their interests.

7. Produce a draft

Have it checked over, preferably by someone with legal expertise. Ensure that all terms are clear and unambiguous, and do not restrict the employee from carrying out or further developing the role.

8. Review the contract

The employee should be made aware that signing the contract is tantamount to a legally binding contract and therefore subject to the law of the land.

Although the employee should not have signed the contract if they are not happy with it, ask them, at a later date, if there is something that they think needs changing. Remember that you can't make any changes to the contract without the employee's consent. Problems that occur elsewhere in the organisation may affect contracts wholesale, so be aware. Keep an eye on the personnel literature for court cases and changes in legislation which may affect current or future contracts.

Dos and don'ts for drawing up a contract of employment

Do

- Take time to prepare by examining the job and the future of the role.
- Get an idea of the law relating to contracts of employment.
- Use clear and unambiguous wording in the contract.

Don't

- Forget to draw on the experiences of your colleagues.
- Cut corners – pay for legal advice if it is not available internally.
- Try to restrain the employee too much – allow for some flexibility in the contract.

Useful reading

Books

Contracts and terms and conditions of employment, Peter Burgess (ed.), London: Institute of Personnel and Development, 1995

Tolley's drafting contracts of employment, Gillian Howard, Croydon: Tolley, 1993

Journal articles

Contracts of employment and implied terms 1. IDS Brief, No 562, April 1996, pp7–10

Particulars of employment, Sarah de Gay, Tolley's Employment Law and Practice, Vol 1 no 4, October 1995, pp29–30

Restraining influences, Olga Aikin, Personnel Management, Vol 26 no 6, June 1994, pp65–66

How to draft an employment contract, Alan Fowler, Personnel Management Plus, Vol 4 no 12, December 1993, pp23–24

Thought starters

- Do you know what is in your contract of employment?
- Have you ever had a problem with your contract of employment? What was it?
- Do you know of any case where a contract of employment has been called into question? What happened?
- Has anyone left your organisation and taken staff/customers with them? Could they have been prevented from doing so?

Organising the Induction of New Recruits

This checklist is designed to assist line managers responsible for the induction of new employees. It makes good sense to help new recruits to integrate as quickly as possible into their new surroundings and to become efficient and effective in their work. Failure to do so can, at the very least, lead to erratic progress, with possible hidden costs such as waste of materials and loss of customers.

The format and content of an induction programme will vary according to the size and type of organisation and the existing knowledge, experience and seniority of the recruit. It must be borne in mind, however, that it is as important to educate the newcomer in the culture, language and standards of the organisation as to train him or her to perform a particular job.

Induction should not be viewed in isolation. It should be treated as an extension of the selection process and the beginning of a continuing staff development programme. Known as orientation in the USA, it often consists of two stages: an organisation-wide programme, usually conducted by the human resource department, and a departmental programme. This checklist concentrates on the second stage.

MCI Standards

This checklist has relevance for the MCI Management Standards: Key Role C - Manage People.

Definition

The purpose of induction is to ensure that new employees:

- are integrated into their working environment as quickly as possible
- learn relevant aspects of the organisation's mission, culture, policies, procedures and methods of working
- become productive and well motivated
- become aware of the skills and knowledge needed for the job
- understand their responsibilities.

Advantages of induction

- Newcomers are integrated more quickly into the organisation and become productive earlier.
- You show that you value the newcomer, making them feel welcome and giving them a sound impression of the organisation.
- Recruitment costs are seen as an investment.
- Successful induction is an essential first stage of an employee development programme.

Action checklist

1. Appoint a mentor

Consider asking someone about the same age and grade of the newcomer to act as a friend and advisor for the first few weeks. This will be particularly useful in a large, complex organisation or in helping to explain the myriad of detail not fully covered elsewhere. Monitor the relationship, however, and step in if it isn't working.

2. Plan the induction and involve and inform others

An induction programme should ideally be drawn up but certainly authorised by the newcomer's manager. The mentor should also be involved in the process. Other staff who will be working with the new employee should be informed of the induction programme whether or not they will be involved. The induction plan should contain three stages: the first day or two should cover the bare essentials; the first three or four weeks should be learning by a mix of approaches; the three to six month period should gradually familiarise the newcomer with all departments.

3. Prepare the work area

Clear and tidy the new employee's work area. Check that all relevant stationery is to hand and equipment is in working order.

4. Introduce the recruit to the organisation and the department

On the first day it is usually the personnel department who informs the newcomer of housekeeping arrangements (where the toilets and the canteen are for example), and covers the sorts of issues contained in the staff handbook (such as salary payments, leave arrangements and sick pay scheme). Make sure that the new employee has copies of any necessary documentation, the organisation chart and job description for example. An introduction to the department and team in which they will be working must also be made. Although the newcomer will be introduced to people around the organisation a detailed look at what other departments do will follow at a later stage of the induction process.

5. Emphasise the importance of organisation policies and procedures

New employees must be made aware at an early stage of policies and regulations based on legislation, eg in the area of health and safety. Other procedures based on national standards, such as IS0 9000, and other schemes, such as internal employee development or mentoring, should also be introduced.

6. Plan a balanced introduction to the work

Whether training is done by the sitting-with-Nellie approach or by professional trainers, a mix of explanation, observation, practice and feedback is advisable. Beware of information overload. The new employee should be given some real work to do to avoid boredom and to give early opportunities for achievement.

7. Clarify performance standards

Make the performance levels you require clear from the outset. An employee cannot be expected to meet standards of which they are unaware.

8. Conduct regular reviews of progress

These should be made during the induction programme, for example, on a weekly basis, to ensure that all the objectives and the new employee's needs are being met. The programme may have to be adapted to match individual learning requirements and speeds. Usually reviews will consist of informal chats but a more formal appraisal interview may take place at the end of the programme, particularly if the employee is on probation. The views of the employee on the overall induction process should be sought for the design of future programmes.

Dos and don'ts for organisations with new recruits

Do

- Ensure that all relevant staff know about and are involved as necessary in the induction process.
- Review a new employee's progress regularly and be prepared to incorporate his or her expressed needs into the induction programme.
- Evaluate the style and content of the induction programme and amend it if necessary, taking into account the views of employees who have had recent experience of it.

Don't

- Forget that starting a new job is a stressful experience for most people.
- Give the employee too much information at once.
- Make assumptions about the recruit's learning and integration.
- Forget that an induction lasts longer than one day or even one week.

Useful reading

Books

Induction: managing best practice 38, London: Industrial Society, 1997

Employee induction: a good start, 3rd ed., Alan Fowler, London: Institute of Personnel and Development, 1996

How to design and deliver induction training programmes, 2nd ed., Michael Meighan, London: Kogan Page, 1995

Effective induction and training: a practical guide to enhanced performance, Larry R Smalley, London: Kogan Page, 1995

Journal articles

Initiative rites, Sheena Wilson, Human Resources UK, no 26, Sep/Oct 1996, pp57–58

Staff entrance, Sarah Heggarty, Personnel Today, 7 Nov 1995, pp31–32

Induction into communication at First Direct, Industrial Relations Review and Report, no 568, Sep 1994, pp8–11

Useful addresses

Industrial Society, 48 Bryanston Square, London W1H 7LN, Tel: 0171 262 2401

The Institute of Management, Cottingham Road, Corby, Northants NN17 1TT, Tel: 01536 204222

Institute of Personnel and Development, IPD House, Camp Road, London SW19 4UX, Tel: 0181 971 9000

Thought starters

- How did you feel in your first days with a new employer?
- How much do early leavers cost your organisation?
- How quickly do new recruits become productive members of the team?

Using Your Staff to Mutual Advantage

This checklist is aimed at managers and looks closely at the building blocks of relationships between those who manage and those whom they manage.

Annual reports frequently pay tribute to 'our staff' but practice seldom seems to match the written word. This checklist will consider some of the major elements involved in getting the most out of working with others, including the changes in management practice in organisations, how change affects people, approaches to leadership and communication, and how to consolidate and improve working relationships.

MCI Standards

This checklist has relevance for the MCI Management Standards: Key Role C – Manage People.

Definition

'Staff' implies any people or group who are subordinate to a manager at any level. 'To mutual advantage' signifies to the advantage of the manager, to the advantage of the unit be it company, department or small firm, and to the advantage of the staff.

Action checklist

1. Recognise the shifts in management practice

In the 1980s and 1990s many organisations moved away from structures which tended to differentiate workers from each other towards more flexible organisational arrangements which used more fully the experience of their people. Often summarised as the empowered, flatter organisation, there are a number of elements discernible in this shift away from practices which, quite simply, no longer work.

This shift was between:

- the autocratic manager and the leader who energises his/her people
- authority by position and authority by merit
- domination and coordination
- control from the top and participation and collaboration
- self-advancement and self-development
- individual responsibility and the shared responsibility of teamwork
- controlling the workforce and giving them freedom
- power and empowerment.

With organisational culture firmly based on trust and initiative rather than on dominance, blame or fear, the onus is now on the manager to become a team-member as well as team-leader.

2. Make change work for you

Be aware of the implications of change and its impact on individuals. For the individuals involved, change will mean moving from the familiar to the unfamiliar, from the known to the unknown. It is essential to be aware of the effects change can have, particularly when it is imposed.

Psychologists have suggested that any substantial change in our lives involves a sequence of stages:

- **shock** – emotional feelings of denial, confusion and disbelief, a sense that all around is crumbling – 'this cannot be happening to me'. Offer understanding and acceptance of the state of shock, convey empathy, create opportunities for grievances to be aired, and encourage the disclosure of feelings.

- **withdrawal or resistance** – an attempt to keep the familiar world intact, a search for ways of avoiding the consequences of change and a struggle to maintain the status quo. Counsel individuals to disclose frustrations and anxieties. Listen with attentiveness and sensitivity.

- **acknowledgement** – a sense of inevitability is accompanied by the recognition of a need to keep in step, of a fear of isolation and rejection by others, of uncertainty and insecurity. Help individuals to acknowledge change by reviewing their appropriate skills, competencies and opportunities for development.

- **adaptation** – this stage is reached when rational acceptance of change is matched by emotional and psychological adjustment. Inner confusion and uncertainty begin to give way as preparations for change take place, anxieties are reduced and practical steps forward identified. Help individuals by involving them in the design of new systems and procedures, in gaining familiarity with new resources and equipment and by getting them to propose new solutions and methods.

Different individuals move through these stages at different rates and in different ways. For some, certain stages are assimilated very rapidly, for others, one stage can prove a great obstacle. Understanding the nature of individual behaviour provides the foundation for working with others and getting them to gain advantage from the constantly changing workplace.

In the last resort, most people don't actually mind change and many welcome it, so long as they recognise why it is necessary and are involved in the process – it should be their change.

3. Define the boundaries to responsibility

People new to a job have a great deal of **dependence** on their line manager, but this dependence will normally diminish as the new job-holder gains in experience and learns the ropes. Allow newcomers to grow and feel their way.

As experience grows and the relationship changes, an **interdependence** evolves and interactions arise when the manager needs information on progress or when consultation is required on specific issues. Get your people to report by exception and to present oral solutions to problems they encounter.

An increasing proportion of the job will be characterised by a clear capacity to self-manage without supervision. Resist the temptation to interfere or over-supervise. Encourage this **independence** and the responsibility that goes with it. 'Freedom with accountability' is the key phrase.

All three of the above elements are present in all jobs. Good practice involves recognising their shifting balance and behaving accordingly.

Whether in a situation of rapid change or solid stability, in an empowered culture or not, it is essential to define the limits to the authority enjoyed by the people who work with you. For example, they cannot be wholly effective if they are confused over which sorts of decision:

- they can take on their own, informing you afterwards
- they can take only after consultation with you
- they should pass on to you.

4. Identify your leadership strategy

If leadership is about quality and effectiveness, change and development, and focus on the future, then this style is associated less and less with directing and instructing and more and more with supporting, coaching and delegating, so that people will own their work and be committed to it. There are various techniques or strategies that help in achieving effectiveness as a leader:

- **Management By Walking Around (MBWA)** – Managers and leaders need to see their main activity as an interactive one – working alongside colleagues where tasks are carried out. MBWA is based on the belief that it is only by getting to know our colleagues and what they do that we can provide appropriate leadership.
- **Work Review** – This is a non-directed relationship designed to help colleagues develop professional skills through the regular process of reflection on experience.
- **Critical Friendship** – The concept of 'Critical Friendship' is sometimes used to describe the nature of the relationship between leader and team. It is essentially an active listening role for the leader in which colleagues can explore and clarify aspects of their work experience. The one-to-one discussion facilitates a deeper understanding of the work issues involved.

5. Give feedback

One of the most effective ways of developing others is to help them reflect on their experience in order to learn from it. Feedback is an informal and highly effective way of promoting this process. It is, however, necessary to be aware of some of the psychological implications of giving others information about themselves and their behaviour. Among the behaviours and responses managers may encounter are:

- difficulty in accepting responsibility for behaviour
- fear of making mistakes
- difficulty with uncertainty and change
- assuming that 'others know best'
- self-doubt and lack of confidence
- reluctance to set personal goals for development
- suspicion of 'experts' and those in positions of authority.

Feedback can be of three basic types:

- **Confirmatory** – giving people information that tells them they are on course and moving successfully towards goals (vital but often neglected).
- **Corrective** – offering information that helps others to get back on course when difficulties are present or things are going wrong (this should always be positive, not negative).
- **Motivating** – giving information that tells people about the consequences of both success and difficulties. This combines confirmatory and corrective feedback; the aim is to provide sufficient information to meet the development needs of the receiver and enable appropriate choices to be made and decisions to be taken.

6. Practise proactive passiveness!

Getting the most out of relationships for all parties can be an exhausting process, where there needs to be a constant watch for feelings of inadequacy, excessive cynicism, inability to express oneself or a sense of being 'plateaued'.

While MBWA, work review and critical friendship may involve substantial changes in behaviour to achieve the desired results, other, more routine techniques should be habitual:

- **active listening**, where the listener attempts to gain insights into the perceptual, intellectual and emotional world of the speaker
- **undivided attention**, away from telephones and other interruptions
- **support**, using suggestions and prompts to check meanings, inviting the speaker to continue and otherwise keeping quietly interested
- **conveying understanding**, using body language to indicate understanding, acceptance and agreement.

Practice is needed in all these – they need to become constant habits, not occasional happenings.

7. Review your relationships

Sit down from time to time and ask 'How are we doing?'. Talk over work routines and objectives so that you know where you stand in relation to others, and they to you. Focus on moving forward so that the individual, the section and the organisation are all gaining mutual advantage.

Useful reading

Personal effectiveness, Alexander Murdock and Carol Scutt, Oxford; Butterworth Heinemann, 1993

Personal effectiveness, Roger Bennett, London: Kogan Page, 1989

Thought starters

- What do my people tell their friends and families about me as their boss?
- What do I do which makes it more difficult for them to do the job I want them to do?
- What can I do to understand better what they want from work?
- Am I using all their talents, skills and capabilities?

Attracting and Retaining Women Returners

This checklist is an introduction for organisations seeking to develop best practice in attracting and retaining women returners. Women returners will make up eighty per cent of new entrants to the labour force over the next decade and organisations will need to develop a range of policies in order to maximise the benefits that these potential employees can bring.

MCI Standards

This checklist has relevance for the MCI Management Standards: Key Role C – Manage People.

Definition

Woman returner is a broad term used to cover any woman returning to paid employment, whether full or part time, after a substantial period away from work, usually taken to care for children or elderly relatives.

Returners are the norm among the female workforce: the full time lifelong career woman with a family is still the exception.

Advantages of attracting women returners

- You will be able to select from a wider pool of talent at a time of continuing skill shortages.
- Women returners offer maturity and experience and are likely to be committed and motivated.
- They are likely to be relatively settled and to offer stability: your recruitment costs will be lower and your retention rates higher.
- They are likely to have good organisational and time management skills and to be well focused.
- Women are especially skilled at multi-tasking, something most men find difficult.

Disadvantages of attracting women returners

- There may be initial costs in providing skills updating or confidence building measures.
- You will need to develop more flexible working practices: it may be difficult to extend these to all sections of the workforce.

Action checklist

1. Develop a clear corporate policy

Set out a clear policy concerned with:

- the recruitment and employment of women returners
- their development and promotion.

Where possible, try to obtain examples of other organisations' policies in this area, and learn from their experiences and those of women returners in your own organisation. Emphasise that the policy is a way of meeting human resource needs and retaining specialist skills, and secure support for it at the highest management level. Communicate the policy to line managers, and define and set up the mechanisms for implementing it.

2. Map the profile of women returners in your workforce

Establish a profile of the jobs, grades and occupations of women returners within the workforce. Use this as a benchmark against which to review the progress of women returners on a yearly basis.

3. Tackle the cultural changes needed to win acceptance of women returners

There may be attitudinal barriers within the organisation to the employment of women returners. Provide training in equal opportunities if it is not already available.

4. Review working practices imaginatively

Investigate ways of introducing more flexible hours and flexible working practices to enable women returners to combine paid employment and family responsibilities: part time; flexi time; job share; term time; and home working. Make flexible working practices available to all employees in order to minimise resistance.

5. Improve employees' access to childcare

Only large organisations will be able to offer subsidised childcare on-site, but you can actively help women returners to find good quality external provision. Consider sharing nursery places with other local employers (for example the local council), buying in places at private nurseries or offering childcare vouchers. Don't neglect out-of-school care for older children: could you become a partner in after-school and holiday play schemes run in conjunction with local authorities or the voluntary sector? Barclays Bank offers a specialist service to employers who want to establish a work-based nursery.

6. Provide parental and caring leave

Modify existing career break schemes to take account of the needs of carers. Provide flexible leave arrangements for those with caring responsibilities for the elderly or disabled. Provide a minimum period of paid parental leave, with the opportunity for employees to take longer periods of unpaid leave.

7. Provide opportunities for appropriate training

Offer the opportunity for induction training to all returners to include confidence building and skills updating. Once they are in employment, provide training which will enable women returners to develop and gain promotion. Consider family responsibilities when arranging training times. The traditional times of breakfast and twilight meetings are particularly difficult for women.

8. Examine the requirements and rules for promotion

Review age limits for recruitment and promotion. Ensure that women returners are not debarred from promotion by unnecessary rules on age, experience or hours of work.

9. Consider extending maternity provision for other women returners

Can you provide maternity rights above the statutory minimum to encourage current employees to return after a break? Offer reasonable maternity rights with the option of a career break without loss of seniority.

10. Set up a 'keeping in touch' scheme

Enable women on maternity leave to follow developments at work. Provide a company sponsor or mentor, and arrange regular mailings with copies of in-house newsletters, magazines and other communications. Make provision for a short period of work and training during each year of absence.

Dos and don'ts for attracting and retaining women returners

Do

- Give attention to how policy developed at corporate level is translated into practice: ensure it is not undermined by line managers.
- Recognise previous experience and informal qualifications and use NVQs as a way of crediting and validating these.
- Enable women returners to enjoy normal career progression by the removal of artificial barriers to promotion.

Don't

- Neglect the training and development needs of those returning to work after a long break: invest in skills updating and confidence building.
- Target flexible working schemes at women returners only, or you will increase cultural resistance.

Useful reading

Beyond the career break, Wendy Hirsh, Brighton: Institute for Manpower Studies, 1992

Women returners' employment potential: an agenda for action, Women's National Commission, London: Cabinet Office, 1991

Good practices in the employment of women returners, Amin Rajan and Penny van Eupen, Brighton: Institute for Manpower Studies, 1990

Useful addresses

Equal Opportunities Commission, Overseas House, Quay Street, Manchester M3 3HN, Tel: 0161 833 9244

Business in the Community, 44 Baker Street, London W1M 1DH, Tel: 0171 629 1600

Women Returners Network, 8 John Adam Street, London WC2N 6EZ, Tel: 0171 839 8188

Advisory, Conciliation and Arbitration Service (ACAS), Brandon House, 180 Borough High Street, London SE1 1LW, Tel: 0171 210 3613. Free advice on the employment of people.

Thought starters

- Are you a woman returner?
- How did your organisation help you?
- What more could have been done?

Introducing Flexible Working into your Organisation

This checklist provides an introduction to the use of flexible working practices within an organisation by considering alternatives to traditional working hours. The introduction of flexibility to the place of work is covered in the Checklist on 'Teleworking' on page 46.

Employers are continually searching for ways to stay 'lean and mean' but effective. Flexibility in working hours is increasingly viewed as a way to manage time and people more effectively within a volatile trading environment, and as a means of recruiting and retaining good people within a more competitive labour market.

MCI Standards

This checklist has relevance for the MCI Management Standards: Key Role A – Manage Activities.

Definition

'Flexibility' covers any variation in working hours other than the standard 9.00 am to 5.00 pm working day. The key variants are: flexible working hours; term time working; annual hours; job sharing; voluntary reduced work time; employment breaks; and sabbaticals. These are defined in the glossary of terms.

Advantages of flexibility

- Recruitment and retention of qualified staff who may not be able to work traditional hours.
- Equality of opportunity: standard hours often prevent women with caring responsibilities or the disabled from working.
- Flexibility in tailoring work patterns to expected peaks and troughs in demand or new customer requirements.
- Greater ability to tackle skills shortages.

- Higher return on training investment.
- **Flexible working hours:**
  - reduce problems of punctuality and of disciplining staff for late arrival
  - reduce one day absenteeism: staff can use flexi-time to deal with minor crises or personal appointments
  - create a greater sense of responsibility and better time management
  - improve efficiency in core times and reduce overtime.
- **Term time working:**
  - facilitates availability to work for people usually with younger children.
- **Annual hours working:**
  - reduces overall number of hours worked and overtime
  - increases productivity by making it easier to manage seasonal variations in work.
- **Job sharing:**
  - two sets of skills/experience applied to one job
  - job sharers can be more energetic, committed and fresher than full time employees
  - greater continuity in cases of sickness or leave.
- **Voluntary reduced work time:**
  - opens up flexible work to a wider range of people.
- **Employment breaks:**
  - retains the service of staff who would otherwise leave the organisation altogether.
- **Sabbaticals:**
  - employees return with greater energy and creativity.

Disadvantages of flexibility

- More management time needed to arrange cover and schedule work.
- If schemes are not handled sensitively and made available to all employees they can generate resentment among full time employees.
- **Flexible working hours:**
  - can encourage people to count the minutes rather than doing the job.
- **Term time working:**
  - can be difficult to provide cover for senior staff during holidays
  - may place an unfair burden on full time staff.
- **Annual working hours:**
  - need to invest more time in scheduling work and anticipating peaks
  - in practice, difficult to control over a long period.
- **Job sharing:**
  - may be communications difficulties
  - can be damaging to continuity if one starts a job and then leaves it to another.

Action checklist

1. Secure the commitment of top management

Reach agreement with senior managers on the extent of flexibility and ensure they are committed to this.

2. Draw up a profile of the existing workforce and their current hours

Unless you do this you may not realise the extent of informal flexible working already sanctioned by line managers.

3. Consider a working group to represent all levels and types of employee

Use the group to steer through the changes and act as a sounding board.

4. Decide how flexible the organisation can afford to be

Are you willing to consider all options for flexibility, or do you want to limit employees to a fixed range? Flexitime, for example, should apply to everyone at all levels. Also, once flexible working is adopted it is difficult to go backwards. Pilot the scheme, and expand it only gradually.

5. Consult all employees

Either seek views on any changes they would like to see or on certain options only: use questionnaires, workshops or discussion groups.

6. Use the working group to consider the options for change

- What system will there be for arranging cover?
- What effect will there be on pay?
- Will you allow line managers discretion in interpreting a broad policy or will there be little scope for variation within a scheme?
- How will you ensure parity of treatment in training and development, promotion and benefits?
- Will there be a qualifying period or age restrictions?
- Will any additional costs be offset by business benefits?

7. Secure senior management agreement to the proposed changes and confirm their commitment

Ensure senior managers are aware of the rationale for introducing flexibility and the business case for it.

8. Communicate the policies to all staff

Publicise the schemes widely. Use existing examples and role models. Be open and honest about terms and conditions of eligibility for each option and set clear guidelines for their use.

9. Identify a co-ordinator

You will need somebody to retain a general overview of the schemes and offer guidance on their implementation.

10. Train line managers/team leaders in implementing the schemes

Continuing management control is vital as flexibility is introduced. It is the manager's job to ensure that work gets done; this may mean restricting what staff may prefer on individual occasions.

11. Set up a system to monitor and evaluate the schemes

Ensure that evaluation is done against the business benefits sought.

12. Consider whether a programme is needed to bring in any changes to culture or attitudes to support the new practices

Dos and don'ts for the effective introduction of flexibility

Do

- Consult staff first.
- Stress the business benefits to line managers at all stages of introduction and implementation.
- Target schemes at all employees.
- Assume that all jobs can be done flexibly unless a business case can be made.

Don't

- Gear the schemes exclusively toward women with children.
- Make assumptions about employees' needs and wishes.

Glossary of terms

Flexible working hours allow employees to choose within set limits the times they start and finish work and normally allow them to carry over any excess of deficit in hours beyond the accounting period (usually four weeks) with the option of taking flexi-leave.

Term time working allows employees to remain on a permanent full or part time contract but gives them the right to unpaid leave of absence during school holidays.

Annual hours working defines the period of time within which employees must work over a whole year: employees will normally be required to work longer hours at certain times of the year to fit any seasonal variations in work-load.

Job sharing allows two people to share the duties of one full time job, dividing pay, holiday and other benefits between them according to the number of hours worked: each job sharer is on a permanent contract with pro-rata pay and benefits.

Voluntary reduced work time schemes allow employees voluntarily to trade income for time off: employees have the option of reducing full time hours by between 5% and 50% for a specified period with the right to return to full time work. Pay and holidays are allocated pro-rata.

Employment breaks are extended periods of unpaid leave for employees who need time away from work but have the intention of returning to a job at the same level. Most schemes have a minimum length of service requirement and a limit on the length of the break.

Sabbaticals are a period of time on full pay, given in addition to annual leave, for those with long service, or in jobs which demand sustained intellectual input.

Useful reading

Flexible working: a strategic guide to successful implementation and operation, S Simons, London: Kogan Page, 1996

Changing times: A guide to flexible work patterns for human resource managers, London: New Ways to Work, 1993

Family Friendly Policies, The Industrial Society, London, 1993

Flexible Working for Managers, Isabel Boyer, London: Chartered Institute of Management Accountants, 1993

Thought starters

- Are you tackling flexible working at the three levels on which change needs to operate – culture, policies and practice?
- Are you making assumptions about what your employees want?
- How will you evaluate the business benefits?

Teleworking

This checklist provides an introduction for line managers wanting to implement teleworking in the organisation for the first time, either as a planned scheme or as an ad hoc response to individual requests.

Many people have always worked from home, but this has traditionally been in low skilled jobs. The development of new computer and telecommunications technology has opened up the opportunity for teleworking to new workers including professional and managerial staff.

MCI Standards

This checklist has relevance for the MCI Management Standards: Key Roles A and B – Manage Activities and Manage Resources.

Definition

Francis Kinsman defines teleworking as remote working, or telecommuting, which entails working somewhere away from the office on either a full time or a part time basis, and communicating with it (usually) electronically rather that commuting to it physically.

Potential advantages of teleworking

- Reducing office overheads or avoiding a move to new or larger premises.
- Making services available to customers outside standard working hours.
- Taking advantage of a ready and cheaper supply of labour in a different locality.
- Reducing the amount of time mobile workers spend in reporting to a central office.
- Basing workers nearer to clients or suppliers.
- Attracting or retaining workers with scarce skills or those with disabilities.
- Retaining trained staff who need flexible arrangements to care for dependants.
- Lowering absenteeism: teleworkers are less likely to take sick leave.
- Improving productivity. Staff are:
  - fresher because they spend less time travelling
  - more reliable, more loyal and likely to spend longer with the organisation
  - likely to take less time off, because they can plan their personal time better.

Disadvantages of teleworking

- Staff can become socially isolated, particularly in routine or mundane jobs. They lack the stimulus of personal contact, and regular feedback for personal assessment and improvement.
- Staff can become demotivated unless there are good communications practices in place.
- New management schemes need to be devised to measure work by output and these can become mechanical.

Action checklist

1. Carry out a feasibility study

Include in the study a cost-benefit analysis. Take into account: productivity; travel; communication and training costs; administrative support requirements; and office space.

2. Decide the basis on which you will introduce teleworking

- A central policy – the option of teleworking is introduced organisation-wide through a formal policy.
- Functional reorganisation – teleworking is selected for a specific function only.
- Self-selection – the teleworkers choose themselves by proposing the arrangement or by creating the situation which leads a manager to suggest it.
- External recruitment – teleworking is introduced for a function and new staff are recruited externally.
- Upgrading mobile staff – staff already employed and mobile are equipped with information technology to allow them to work partially from home.

3. Conduct a pilot and evaluate the results

A pilot may not be needed if teleworking is introduced on an ad hoc basis for individual jobs but is essential before it is brought in throughout the organisation.

4. Decide which individual jobs are suitable for teleworking

The work must be intrinsically interesting and not too monotonous. It must be capable of being carried out without continuous face to face contact with others and of being measurable by results.

5. Select the individual teleworkers

Working from home requires special personal qualities in addition to the normal criteria for the job, including: maturity; trustworthiness; self-sufficiency and self-discipline, and good time management and communications skills. Some of these may need to be developed.

6. Prepare teleworkers and their managers

Ensure the home environment is suitable: i.e. peaceful and safe. Give clear information about how to deal with isolated working conditions. Consider workshops for new teleworkers and mentoring or shadowing schemes.

7. Put the right communications structures in place

Do you need electronic mail or a more efficient messaging system? Are the ground rules clear on how and when the teleworker is expected to communicate?

8. Provide suitable equipment

Most equipment is normally supplied by the employer and includes: suitable desk, chair and storage facilities; telephone and dedicated line; fax and answering machine; personal computer; printer, and modem. Ensure equipment is ergonomically sound, fully compatible with systems used elsewhere in the organisation, easy to use and easily maintained. If appropriate equipment is already held by the teleworker, then arrangements should be put in place for payment for use and maintenance.

9. Ensure equipment is safeguarded

Take out a service contract on all equipment and provide access to technical helplines. Install anti-virus software and ensure teleworkers only use software supplied by the organisation and that they have effective back-up systems. Ensure the employee has insurance or arrange it.

10. Draw up a contract

Many teleworkers have permanent employee status and only need additional clauses in a standard contract which might cover: expected working hours, including any 'core time'; reporting procedures; equipment responsibilities; health and safety; and details of recoverable expenses or allowances.

11. Consider whether additional training is needed

The teleworker may need to improve generic skills, for example, keyboard skills, use of software and hardware, report-writing, communications or time management.

12. Provide facilities for teleworkers on office days

Ensure that if teleworkers are required to attend the office on certain days they have access to necessary facilities: telephone; computer terminal; and personal filing. These can be shared among several teleworkers ('hot desks').

13. Set up support systems for teleworkers

Try to create a sense of belonging. Ensure teleworkers receive organisational newsletters and publications and details of relevant training courses and social events. Mentoring may also be appropriate in some cases.

14. Set up effective management systems

Teleworkers will need to be managed by results. Set up a performance measurement system if one is not already in place. Ensure teleworkers are included in staff appraisal and development systems.

15. Establish a monitoring system

Ensure review mechanisms are in place to pick up costs and benefits and assess where adaptations are needed.

16. Arrange regular meetings

Regular meetings, every six months for example, between teleworkers and managers can provide the framework for motivation, control and review.

Dos and don'ts for effective teleworking

Do

- Be convinced of the business benefits of teleworking before it is introduced.
- Find ways of motivating and providing social contact for teleworkers whose job involves little interaction with people.
- Ensure line managers are in at least daily contact with teleworking staff.
- Provide adequate training in handling new equipment and ensure back-up services.
- Make teleworking available at all levels and within all suitable functions.
- Review the staff and the jobs open to teleworking on a regular basis.

Don't

- Consider teleworking as an alternative to child care.
- Make assumptions about which staff will want to become teleworkers.
- Leave teleworkers isolated.

Useful reading

Teleworking: guidelines for good practice, Ursula Huws and others, Brighton: Institute for Employment Studies, 1997
Teleworking in brief, Mike Johnson, Oxford: Butterworth Heinemann, 1997
Teleworking: a directors guide, Director Publications, 1996
A manager's guide to teleworking, Employment Department Group, London: 1995
Making telecommuting happen, Jack M Niles, New York: Van Nostrand Reinhold, 1994
Teleworking, IDS Study, December 1996, no 616, whole issue
Teleworking explained, Mike Gray, Noel Hodson and Gil Gordon, Chichester: John Wiley, 1993

Useful addresses

Teleworking Special Interest Group, c/o The Virtual Office, 211 Piccadilly, London W1V 9LD
National Association of Teleworkers, The Island House, Midsomer Norton, Bath BA3 2HL
New Ways to Work, 309 Upper Street, London N1 2TY
The Telecottage Association, WREN Telecottage, Stoneleigh Park CV8 2RR

Thought starters

- What business objectives do you want to achieve by introducing teleworking?
- If driven by cost-savings alone what business benefits, or disadvantages, may accrue?
- Do benchmark organisations have a teleworking track record?
- If you have ever worked from home yourself what were the advantages or problems?

Setting Up Childcare Policies

This checklist provides guidance for those responsible for the implementation of a childcare policy within an organisation. It focuses on the general principles and considerations involved; specific policy options, such as workplace nurseries or childcare vouchers, are described in the Glossary of terms.

The provision of help with childcare is increasingly viewed as a valuable benefit by employees, as it assists them in balancing work and domestic responsibilities. On the employer's side, childcare is seen as a means of retaining staff and contributing towards equal opportunities objectives.

MCI Standards

This checklist has relevance for the MCI Management Standards: Key Roles B and C – Manage Resources and Manage People.

Definition

A childcare policy is a voluntary scheme put into practice by the employer to provide, or to help to provide, care for the children of employees during working hours. The aim of such a policy is to enable primary carers to return to work despite childcare responsibilities. Care may be provided for children of all ages and can be implemented in a single scheme, or as a combination of a number of childcare options (see the Glossary of terms). To comply with equal opportunities legislation, childcare provision has to be made available to both male and female employees.

Advantages of setting up childcare policies

- Experienced and skilled staff are able to return to/continue in work, reducing recruitment and training costs.
- A wider range of applicants may be attracted for vacant positions.
- The image of the firm is enhanced, as it is seen to be a caring and employee-friendly organisation.

Workplace nurseries

- Parent and child are on site allowing access for parents to their children at lunchtimes or in emergencies.
- Workplace nurseries are a tax-free benefit.
- Nurseries can provide a beneficial environment for children.

Buying places at local nurseries

- Start-up costs for employers are eliminated.
- Nursery management responsibilities are avoided.

Childcare allowances

- These are much cheaper than paying for nursery provision and can be used in the parents' local area.
- Parents are able to choose the form of childcare they prefer.

Childcare vouchers

- They can purchase almost any form of childcare.
- They can only be cashed in exchange for childcare.
- They are subject to a number of tax benefits for employers and employees.
- They can be used in the parents' local area.

Information/Advisory services

- These are low cost schemes which require less management and administration to run than other options.

Disadvantages of setting up childcare policies

- Staff without children may feel resentful of benefits they will not receive.

Workplace nurseries

- They are expensive to set up and run.
- They must be registered with the local authority's social services department and are subject to annual inspection.
- Not all parents would wish, or find it possible, to commute with their children to work every day.
- Facilities have to be found to house the nursery within the building or nearby, which could prove costly and deny space to other departments in the organisation.

Buying places at local nurseries

- This option can be expensive and may be considered a taxable benefit.
- Nurseries where places have been bought may not be convenient for all.

Childcare allowances

- These are subject to tax and national insurance.
- Administration is needed to establish selection criteria for employees entitled to financial assistance.
- There is no guarantee that the allowance will be spent on childcare.

Childcare vouchers

- Service charges have to be paid to the issuing company.
- Their usefulness is limited if there is inadequate childcare provision in the area where the recipients of vouchers live.

Action checklist

1. Examine the short term and long term needs of the firm for the provision of childcare

Will a childcare policy benefit the organisation in the long term justifying high initial costs? Is there a demand for a childcare policy?

2. Obtain the full commitment of top management to the implementation of a childcare policy and appoint a project team

Without overt commitment from the top, the policy has little chance of success. Establish who will be responsible for the implementation and management of the policy. This is important, as the implementation of a childcare policy is a long term commitment and quality of provision is essential. Consequently the individuals involved must be prepared to be scheme champions. A project team should be assembled to collect and assess information and help formulate policy. This should include a member of the Personnel Department.

3. Ascertain all the policy options available

Ensure that the implications of each policy are thoroughly researched, including: costs; legal regulations; which options are and are not available in the immediate vicinity of the workplace; and the location of the workforce in relation to the workplace.

4. Consult employees

Having decided which options would be practical to implement, present them to employees and survey their attitudes to the choices open to them. Which policy would they prefer and why?

5. Formulate policy

Taking the views of employees into full account, and the requirements and preferences of the firm, choose one, or a combination, of the options.

6. Draw up a business plan detailing policy

Set time scales for implementation, and estimate implementation and ongoing costs. Ensure that regulations governing each method of childcare provision are adhered to and that all relevant organisations are kept informed of the implementation of policy. The scope of provision should be outlined in the plan. Establish the rate of any fees / allowances / contributions. If applicable, decide the range of hours provision will cover, and ascertain any limits in numbers of employees who will be covered by provision.

7. Launch the scheme

Inform employees of the final childcare policy decision some time in advance of the scheme's launch, as many parents in work will already have made childcare arrangements with family, friends or providers of childcare in their area. After the launch, allow time for parents to adjust to the service, and for numbers of participants in the scheme to increase.

8. Review the scheme

Assess and monitor standards continuously to ensure that childcare policies meet the needs of the organisation, the employees and their children.

Dos and don'ts for setting up childcare policies

Do

- Recognise that a childcare policy is a long term commitment.
- Plan thoroughly, exploring every childcare option available.
- Seek advice on legal and financial implications of any policy decision.

Don't

- Rush planning or implementing a childcare policy.
- Impose a policy on staff without consulting them.
- Expect immediate, quantifiable results.

Glossary of terms

Workplace nurseries are usually on site or located in nearby premises provided by the employer. They can be run in-house or by a contractor who specialises in nursery care provision. Some organisations work in partnership with another firm to provide nursery facilities, thus sharing the costs and management responsibilities.

Purchased places in nurseries enable employers to provide their employees with guaranteed places in local nurseries for their children. In some cases the costs are absorbed by the firm, in others they are passed on to the employee.

Childcare allowances are paid directly to the individual employee in the form of a cash payment, or are placed in a childcare fund.

Childcare vouchers work in a similar way to luncheon vouchers and are issued by Childcare Vouchers Ltd, a division of Luncheon Vouchers Ltd. Employers obtain vouchers up to a certain value, which they then distribute to employees who need them. Vouchers can obtain any form of childcare provision and the provider then redeems them from the issuer at face value.

Information services can be run in-house or contracted out to specialist consultancies. They provide information and advice on the childcare options available to parents and the providers of care in the local area. Employees then decide which type of childcare they wish to obtain.

Holiday/After school provision enables parents, who have children of school age and whose hours of work do not correspond with school times, to obtain care. Such schemes can make additional use of day nurseries, or take advantage of local playschemes in the area. These are often run by local councils, church groups or local clubs and societies. A government initiative provides funding distributed through local TECs for those establishing out-of-school group provision.

Flexible working means that the working hours for employees deviate from the 9-5 norm. Options include flexible working hours, term time working, job share schemes and voluntary reduced work time.

Useful reading

Close to home: family friendly services, Julia Carter, London: London Enterprise Agency, 1995

A practical guide to childcare for personnel managers, Sue Finch, London: Working for Childcare, 1993

Childcare providers, IDS Personnel Products and Services, March 1996

Childcare, IDS Study, no 574, March 1995

Useful addresses

Childcare Association, 8 Talbot Road, London N6 4QR, Tel: 0181 348 2800

National Childcare Campaign, 4 Wild Court, London WC2B 4AU, Tel: 0171 405 5617

National Childminding Association, 8 Masons Hill, Bromley, Kent BR2 9EY, Tel: 0181 464 6164

Childcare Vouchers Ltd and Childcare Solutions, 50 Vauxhall Bridge Road, London SW1V 2RS, Tel: 0171 834 6666

Thought starters

- What is your labour turnover rate?
- How many people with childcare responsibilities leave? How much does it cost to replace them?
- Do you know people in your organisation who would value help with childcare?

Introducing an Equal Opportunities Policy

This checklist provides managers with the basis for introducing an equal opportunities policy. Increasingly, such a policy is a moral, legal and business imperative for all line managers.

MCI Standards

This checklist has relevance for the MCI Management Standards: Key Roles A and C – Manage Activities and Manage People.

Definition

An equal opportunities policy is a commitment by the organisation to the development of procedures and practices which provide genuine equality of opportunity for all employees, regardless of sex, marriage, ethnic origin or disability. Its remit goes beyond strict compliance with the law and ensures the effective use of all human resources within the organisation.

Advantages of an equal opportunities policy

- The ability to attract people with new ways of thinking; leading to a more diverse work-force with a richer mix of skills and experience.
- The ability to attract the best talent.
- A more stable work-force which retains the best people by ensuring their needs are fully met.
- An improved reputation for the company through higher ethical standards.

Disadvantages of an equal opportunities policy

- A dissatisfied work-force if raised expectations are not met in full.
- Higher recruitment and monitoring costs.
- Resentment or 'backlash' among previously privileged groups of the work-force.

Action checklist

1. Secure the commitment of top management

Demonstrate that the organisation is serious about equal opportunities by giving overall responsibility to a senior manager, preferably at board level.

2. Designate a post with specific responsibility for introducing and implementing equal opportunities

Appoint an equal opportunities officer to coordinate actions on a day to day basis. Define the responsibilities and level of responsibility clearly even if the post need not be full time.

3. Establish a working party to provide employee input

Set up a working party drawn from representative groups within the organisation including union or staff associations, management, personnel, women and ethnic minority groups and the disabled. Make it clear that the group is not a lobbying point for special interest groups.

4. Review policies adopted by other organisations

Obtain copies of the policies of other organisations in the same sector. Draw on these to prepare a first draft of your own policy. Take care to include only objectives and commitments that are appropriate to your culture and attainable within a realistic timescale.

5. Decide the scope of your policy and distinguish between law and good practice

The law covers only discrimination on the grounds of sex or race (including ethnic origin) and, since 1995, disability. It does not cover age, class, sexuality or religion (except in Northern Ireland). However, most policies, while laying down what people must not do in terms of the law, go further and include good practice about what they should do. Make clear in yours where it is underpinned by law and where employees will be held legally liable for their actions.

6. Conduct an 'equality audit' to establish a baseline for action

Conduct a workplace audit to provide information about the composition of the work-force in relation to gender, race and disability. If the information is not already held in personnel records, carry out an employment survey but make it clear that the information collected will be used only for equal opportunity purposes. Review how many women and men you employ: in total, by grade and salary, by hours of work, by marital/family status and by ethnic origin. Use this information to identify existing patterns of employment and under-representation.

7. Draw up a programme of action

Use the information captured to identify the areas for attention within the organisation. Consider whether you will require positive action: both the Sex and Race Discrimination Acts allow certain steps to redress the effects of past discrimination and to level out the playing field for the future. At a minimum, the programme will need to cover: recruitment, selection, induction, flexible working, assistance for careers and training.

8. Set targets for under-represented groups

UK law allows employers to set a numerical objective for the groups which have previously been under-represented in the workforce; for example, that 30% of line managers should be women by the year 2005. Set targets that are challenging enough to stretch the organisation to change but realistic enough to show existing employees they have a fair chance of promotion.

9. Provide equal opportunities training

Provide specific equal opportunities training first to priority groups such as senior executives, personnel specialists, recruiters and selectors, reception staff and other 'gate keepers'. Where applicable, these groups should then cascade training through line managers to all employees.

10. Offer flexible working arrangements to employees of all grades, such as part time work, flexi time, job sharing and term-time working

Assume that all jobs can be done on a flexible basis unless there is a clear occupational requirement for a full-time employee. Ensure that flexibility in hours is available to all employees – not just to women.

11. Review job descriptions

Re-write all job descriptions objectively when a vacancy arises, based on the organisation's needs, not on the needs or preferences of the person currently doing the job.

12. Review selection and recruitment practices

Shortlist candidates only on the basis of whether they meet essential skills and knowledge requirements of the job, rather than personal characteristics. Remove personal details (such as name, date of birth, nationality and marital status) from applications before they are seen by selectors.

13. Provide parental, family or adoptive leave and career breaks to female and male employees and assistance with child and elder care

Offer schemes for parental leave, child care and flexible working to all employees, not just to enable female staff to combine work and family; otherwise they are unlawful.

14. Regularly review the existing qualifications and training needs of all employees

Monitor take-up of training by different categories of employee. Where necessary, make special training available for employees who have traditionally been discriminated against.

15. Ensure your training programmes provide for comparable on and off the job training for all employees at every level

Distinguish between training to improve job performance and training to acquire new skills. Make clear the links between acquiring new skills and the possibility of regrading.

16. Introduce a written and accessible grievance procedure which is widely publicised and which employees can use to pursue allegations of gender discrimination, harassment or equal pay

Assume all allegations are well-founded while they are being investigated and deal promptly and openly with them.

17. Introduce monitoring and review procedures

Your equality audit will only give details of your current work-force. Set up monitoring systems, to capture details of all job applicants and those recruited; and establish performance indicators to review progress against your targets and action plan. Monitor internal and external appointments by gender, marital status and ethnic origin: you may also want to include age.

18. Communicate policies and practices clearly

Send a copy of the policy to potential and actual applicants, new recruits and existing employees. Use every opportunity to publicise the policy, including company literature.

Dos and don'ts for introducing an effective equal opportunities policy

Do

- Consult employees and trade union representatives.
- Use positive action measures to meet your equality targets.
- Monitor and review progress annually against the targets and consider whether positive action is needed.
- Beware of bias in interview techniques.

Don't

- Set unrealistically high targets.
- Fall into the trap of positive discrimination.
- Target flexible work and child care schemes only at women.

Useful reading

Racial equality means business: a standard for racial equality for employers, London: Commission for Racial Equality, 1995
Gender Equality Checklist, Manchester: Equal Opportunities Commission, 1994
Equal opportunities: a practical handbook, Gillian Taylor, London: Industrial Society, 1994
Fair recruitment and selection, Gerard Lemos, London: Lemos Associates, 1994

Useful addresses

Equal Opportunities Commission, Overseas House, Quay Street, Manchester, M3 3HN, Tel: 0161 833 9244
Commission for Racial Equality, Elliot House, 10-12 Allington Street, London, SW1E 5EH, Tel: 0171 828 7022

Glossary

Targets are forecasts of the percentage of ethnic minority, women or disabled employees that employers realistically aim to have by a specific date. Targets are generally lawful in the UK.
Quotas are a fixed percentage of posts reserved for a particular group. They are generally unlawful in the UK.
Positive discrimination means discriminating in favour of someone from a previously disadvantaged group because he or she is a woman or of a particular ethnic origin. It is illegal in the UK, except in exceptional circumstances and where there is a 'Genuine Occupational Qualification' (very limited exemptions which allow you to recruit from a particular racial group or sex – for example, where authenticity is required in the serving of food or drink)
Positive (or affirmative) action involves taking action to promote equality of opportunity in access to a post for a previously disadvantaged group (eg special training to allow ethnic minorities to compete on more equal terms for a particular type or level of work such as management). Positive action is legal

in the UK, provided the employer does not guarantee a job or promotion at the end of it.

Direct racial discrimination occurs if a person is unfavourably treated on racial grounds. These are widely defined to include: colour, ethnic or national origin, race or nationality.

Indirect racial discrimination occurs when a requirement or condition is applied with which only a 'considerably smaller proportion' of persons in different racial groups can comply (eg accepting only British qualifications).

Direct sex discrimination occurs if a person is treated unfavourably because: she is a woman; he is a man.

Indirect sex discrimination consists of applying to a woman a condition or requirement the same as that for a man but which is a condition that only a small number of women would be able to comply with.

Implementing a Diversity Management Programme

This checklist provides a framework for setting up a diversity management programme in an organisation. It is aimed at managers in all areas and at all levels.

Definition

The concept of diversity encompasses any sort of difference between two or more people. Differences might exist in terms of race, age, gender, disability, geographic origin, family status, education, social background – in fact, anything that can affect workplace relationships and achievement. The management of diversity involves the implementation of strategies through which a network of varied individuals are knitted together into a dynamic workforce.

The approach goes beyond that of equal opportunities by recognising an infinite number of differences between people and focusing on the individual rather than various disadvantaged groups. Recognition of diversity within the workforce enables a more positive use of a major organisational resource – people.

Advantages of diversity management

A diversity management programme will encourage compliance with legal requirements covering discriminatory behaviour in the workplace. It will enable an organisation to keep pace with social and demographic changes, such as increasing numbers of female, ethnic minority and older workers in the labour market.

Employee recognition can lead to empowerment, motivation and commitment, and therefore to competitive advantage for the organisation. By encouraging the individual talents of each person it strengthens the pool of human resources on which a company can draw.

Since diversity management encourages employees to feel more valued and more content in their work, labour turnover is lower and savings on recruitment and training costs are made.

A diverse workforce is better equipped to serve a diverse customer base and diverse markets. It also facilitates entry into the global marketplace. Diversity management can create a flexible workforce, which can be more productive. Successful diversity management can benefit corporate image.Diversity management can underpin an organisation's social responsibility.

Disadvantages of diversity management

- If handled insensitively, a diversity programme may invade employees' privacy.
- Implementation of a diversity programme may, in the short term, be expensive.
- Deep-seated prejudices may be brought into the open, causing short-term tension.
- Conflict and ill-feeling may result from a poorly handled programme.

Action checklist

1. Gain top level support

Approach the directors and managers in your organisation and convince them of the advantages of diversity management. Present both the business and social cases for a diversity initiative. If necessary, conduct high level diversity awareness training to develop the commitment of key decision makers.

2. Assign financial and human resources to the programme

Don't underestimate the time and money that will be needed, and look to the long term – the programme will spread over years rather than months. At this stage, identify as many facilitators as possible who can act as change agents to lead the initiative and cascade it throughout the organisation.

3. Decide what you want the programme to achieve and set goals accordingly

Methods used to produce diversity management goals could include consultation, brainstorming, benchmarking, or literature reviews. Ensure that goals are specific and achievable. Examples might be:

- increase the proportion of women in our workforce to 50%
- enable parents to take time off to care for children when they are ill
- facilitate recruitment from a wider geographical area.

Gain the support of employees for these goals, and relate them to the organisation's overall vision and mission statements, and to any other initiatives which are going on in the organisation, such as quality management.

4. Establish current levels of diversity management in your organisation

Plan and conduct a diversity audit to gauge existing levels of diversity management. You will need to assess both qualitative and quantitative evidence, focusing on people, processes and strategies.

Find out:

- which kinds of difference affect the ability of individuals to achieve their working potential in your organisation
- to what extent these differences create disadvantages or advantages for employees
- how the procedures and strategies of the organisation affect different groups of employees.

Some data gathering methods include:

- questionnaires – design these with your target audience in mind, and ensure anonymity and privacy for respondents.
- individual and group interviews – consider who should conduct these and how to create an informal and frank atmosphere.
- focus group discussions – you could, for example, talk to groups of female, disabled, ethnic minority or older employees.
- unobtrusive observation – a discreet walkabout can be very revealing.
- document surveys – examine written procedures, personnel records, customer complaints, publicity material and any other documentary evidence within the organisation.
- benchmarking – look in organisations similar to your own for examples of best practice to follow and of bad practice to avoid.

5. Conduct a gap analysis

Review the audit results and establish how great the difference is between your current position and your goals.

6. Identify areas where change is needed

Work out the forms of action which will be needed to achieve your goals. You may need to make changes to:

- processes – for example, revising the recruitment procedure
- working arrangements – for example, introducing flexi-time, childcare facilities, time off for family responsibilities

- attitudes – for example, combating inter-cultural prejudice and improving inter-cultural communication
- physical environment – for example, creating better access for disabled workers and customers, introducing interdepartmental rest rooms, revising office layout.

7. Write a diversity policy

Use these broad change ideas together with your diversity goals to compile a concise written diversity policy. The policy could cover:

- a definition of diversity
- reasons why it is important
- the goals of the diversity management programme
- the ways in which the goals will be achieved.

Communicate the policy to employees and all stakeholders. Post a copy on every staff noticeboard, in the staff handbook, and, if you have one, on the company intranet.

8. Compile a detailed diversity action plan

Define the finer details of the programme, specifying exactly how the planned changes will be brought about. Hold brainstorming sessions to produce ideas for action, then compose an implementation plan which coordinates and timetables the action to be taken. Make sure the plan includes regular reviews – decide what should be measured and monitored before the programme starts and make data gathering an ongoing part of the plan.

9. Set the programme in motion

Communicate the plan to employees and put it into action. Appoint programme coordinators and publicise their role, giving employees a point for feedback and information.

10. Monitor and review

Monitor the programme over twelve months, and adjust the plan as necessary. Where problems occur, review the diversity policy and decide whether it should be amended.

11. Establish an ongoing programme

Schedule an ongoing diversity programme for the long term. Allow for the programme to be fluid and develop as the organisation's internal and external contexts change. Make sure that diversity remains a high profile issue and work towards its internalisation within the organisation. Diversity management should become a natural part of everyday life.

Dos and don'ts for successfully managing diversity

Do

- Communicate at all stages of the programme. Ensure that employees, managers, customers, shareholders, and other stakeholders are kept informed, as their support is vital to the programme's success.
- Involve everyone. This is not just an issue for the personnel department or senior managers but should concern people throughout the organisation.
- Make use of established change management processes to carry through the programme.
- Look to the long term. Changes which involve attitudes will not happen overnight, and you should expect the programme to last for years rather than weeks or months.
- Be prepared to invest money, time and resources to achieve your goals.

Don't

- Mistake equal opportunities for diversity management. The equal opportunities approach will form a part of any diversity initiative but the programme should go far beyond traditional equal opportunities issues.
- Design the diversity goals and policies for 'them'. Look instead at 'us'. Diversity is about inclusiveness, and you should aim the programme at everyone in the organisation – including yourself!

Useful reading

Diversity in action: managing the mosaic, 2nd ed., Rajvinder Kandola and Johanna Fullerton, London: Institute of Personnel and Development, 1998

Redefining diversity, R Roosevelt Thomas, New York: AMACOM, 1996

Beyond race and gender: unleashing the power of your total workforce by managing diversity, R Roosevelt Thomas, New York: AMACOM, 1991

Implementing diversity, Marilyn Loden, Chicago: Irwin, 1996

Designing and implementing successful diversity programs, Laurence M. Baytos,Englewood Cliffs: Prentice Hall, 1995

Managing cultural diversity at work, Khizar Humayun, Ansari and June Jackson, London: Kogan Page, 1994

Thought starters

- List ten differences between yourself and a close colleague and consider how these differences affect your working life.
- In what ways, if any, does your organisation cater for these differences?
- Could your working arrangements, working environment, company policies and procedures be improved to lessen any negative effects caused by these differences?
- Do you feel respected as an individual in your workplace?
- Is this respect evident from all levels of the organisation?

Implementing a Job Evaluation Scheme

This checklist offers guidance on implementing a job evaluation scheme. It does not explain the detail of the various approaches to job evaluation.

Job evaluation aims to:

- **establish a fair and workable system of differentials between various jobs in the organisation**
- **sort out anomalies between similar jobs in different parts of the same organisation**
- **review the jobs in an organisation, which have changed over time**
- **assess the value of a job that is hard to fill.**

Job evaluation is a specialised process usually handled by human resource specialists. Line managers, however, have a large role to play in helping to define jobs, and in implementing the results.

MCI Standards

This checklist has relevance for the MCI Management Standards: Key Roles B and C – Manage Resources and Manage People.

Definition

Job evaluation is concerned with the worth of a job, especially in relation to other jobs in the organisation. It is not about the individual jobholder, their competence or their potential; nor is it primarily about pay rates, although it may influence pay structures.

Simple approaches towards job evaluation tend to be non-analytical. For example, one method takes one job as the benchmark against which all others are assessed; certain factors in a job are examined in comparison with the benchmark. Another method is to define a grading structure first, then review job specifications within that framework and make any adjustments.

More analytical approaches tend to involve factor weighting and point scoring systems. Each job will be assessed on a number of key factors, such as the size of the budget controlled, the number of staff reporting to the post, direct interface with customers, the level of technical expertise required and the potential impact on the organisation's success. Points are awarded for each factor from a predetermined set of specifications (for example, 5 points if there are 4 or fewer staff reporting, 12 points in the case of 5-15 staff, 20 points in the case of 16-50 and so on) and a total reached which provides the final level of importance. This is then reviewed to take into account any further points of detail that have additional impact on the job's value.

Advantages of job evaluation schemes

Such schemes:

- provide a relatively objective and unbiased view of the worth of jobs
- avoid favouritism or patronage as they take no account of individual job-holders
- iron out current discrepancies and help to prevent future anomalies, which can cause bad feeling, resentment and demands for parity from those who feel they are undervalued
- provide a transparent approach to valuing jobs once established.

Disadvantages of job evaluation schemes

- The process can be lengthy and costly to plan, introduce and implement, especially if an analytical approach is taken and an external consultancy is retained.
- There can be an emotional backlash if the scheme is not introduced with adequate consultation and communication.
- Schemes require adequate representation from all grades and specialisms – individuals should have no grounds for complaint that they feel misunderstood or remote.

Action checklist

1. Carry out some background research

Before starting, it is crucial to think through all the implications and make sure that job evaluation is the route you wish to follow and, if so, whether you are going to adopt an analytical or a non-analytical approach.

- Decide what you want a job evaluation scheme to achieve but keep an open mind, as it may bring other issues to light.
- Consider whether there is an easier and more direct way of tackling the issue, especially if you are facing a small problem of inconsistency, but make sure that your alternative solution will be adequate.

- Try to find one or more colleagues in other organisations with experience of the process.
- If you are planning to use a detailed and analytical approach, research it thoroughly; talk to consultants and read up about it – this is not a route to be followed lightly.
- Once you have all the information, carry out a detailed cost-benefit analysis to identify whether the costs of undertaking job evaluation are outweighed by the benefits. If the benefits are significantly greater than the costs, move on to the next part of the checklist. If not, go back and think through more appropriate ways of achieving your objectives.

2. Decide on the approach

Based on the cost-benefit analysis, decide whether to bring in a consultant with an analytical process, or to do what you can on your own on a less complex basis.

Having chosen the approach, plan the steps carefully and consider all the essential details, such as:

- whether job descriptions are all up-to-date or work is needed to amend them, as they form a major element of job evaluation
- who will be managing the process in-house, either as the prime mover or as the contact point for an external consultant
- how much time you have
- how much it will cost (even if it is controlled internally, because it takes time and resources)
- whether you can afford it now, or whether it is preferable to wait and build it in as a major project in the coming year.

3. Communicate and consult

Think carefully about what impression any announcement will give to staff. Damage control at the start is preferable to damage limitation later. Find out what others will read into the introduction of job evaluation.

Consult wherever it is appropriate; nothing gives more trouble than a false impression or a rumour, so if you will need to talk to unions at some stage, start now; sell the benefits and try to work towards an agreement, which both sides can at least live with.

Communicate so that all staff are clear about what is happening, why, when, and with what aim, and who is doing it.

4. Draw up a project plan

Remember that there are three basic elements to the process of job evaluation:

- scheme design
- data collection
- data analysis.

List and time all actions so you know what comes when, what must precede each action and what depends on it, and the key milestones along the way.

Draw up a separate plan for how you are going to manage change issues, as the scheme will constitute a fairly significant change. Consider its implications in terms of managing change:

- What sort of resistance are you likely to encounter?
- Which factors are helping you and which are going to block you?
- Whom can you pick as change agents or champions to help spread the word?

5. Implement the scheme

If you are using an experienced external consultant, they will be able to advise you on what has to be done and how to go about it. If you are paying for their expertise, make sure you use it.

If you are handling the scheme in-house, follow the project and change management plans; if they were well thought-out at the planning stage, they should work now.

6. Monitor the scheme

After a lengthy haul of design and implementation, be wary of the scheme taking on a life of its own and becoming rigid. Just as jobs will continue to evolve or change, so their content will impact on the scheme framework you have devised.

Ensure you maintain the scheme as jobs change and new ones are created. You may need a panel or team, trained in job evaluation techniques, to meet regularly to carry out re-evaluations.

Dos and don'ts for implementing a job evaluation scheme

Do

- Be aware that, under sex discrimination and equal pay legislation, jobs must be seen to be neutral. There should be absolutely no unfairness or discrimination based on whether men or women happen to be the main group of jobholders.
- Consider using an external consultant – it may seem costly but they can take a great deal of the strain and work off your shoulders and they contribute specialised knowledge and experience.
- Consult and communicate.

Don't

- Imagine that job evaluation will automatically save money; it is a process designed to sort out relativities and positions within an overall structure rather than limiting pay.
- Forget that even the most analytical system needs judgement and a human touch to refine scientific results and make them workable.

Useful reading

The job evaluation handbook, Michael Armstrong and Angela Baron, London: Institute of Personnel and Development, 1995

The role of job evaluation, Jim Hillage, Brighton: Institute of Manpower Studies, 1994

Job evaluation in the 1990s: a directory of schemes and a review of current practice, Fiona Neathey, London: Industrial Relations Review, 1994

Job roles and people: the new world of job evaluation, Derek Pritchard and Helen Murlis, London: Nicholas Brealey, 1992

Job evaluation: an introduction, Advisory, Conciliation and Arbitration Service, London: ACAS, 1989

Thought starters

- Have there been changes in the nature, structure and design of the jobs in your organisation?
- Are there people in your organisation who apparently have the same levels of responsibility but are paid differently?
- Would you have the time and resources available to tackle job evaluation yourself?

Setting Up a Performance-Related Pay Scheme

This checklist is for those whose task it is to establish a performance-related pay scheme.

Implementing Performance-Related Pay (PRP) is by no means a total solution for motivating employees and increasing productivity, as it is widely recognised that for most people money is not the most important aspect of a job. Opinions differ greatly between organisations over the effectiveness of PRP – many organisations have tried PRP, only to abandon it later. Whenever PRP is used, it should be in conjunction with other methods to improve employee performance.

MCI Standards

This checklist has relevance for the MCI Management Standards: Key Roles B and C – Manage Resources and Manage People.

Definition

Performance-related pay links additional payments, over and above basic salary and cost of living increases, to an assessment of an individual's performance. Each employee is set targets or objectives at the beginning of the year and then assessed on them at the end. Depending on how well they did, they are awarded a sum of money which is paid on top of the next year's salary.

Performance-related pay is appropriate both for individuals and teams. This checklist will concentrate on individual PRP.

Advantages of PRP

By relating pay to performance:

- an individual's performance can be raised
- a strong link can be created between a company's goals and objectives and an employee's goals and objectives

- retention and recruitment of staff can be improved – employees will be seen to be rewarded for their efforts.

Disadvantages of PRP

Performance-related pay:

- may lead to over-competitiveness between staff and work against a team culture
- can mean managers ignore informal staff development and performance improvement
- may be assessed differently from manager to manager
- requires a great deal of time and resources to administer.

Action checklist

1. Designate a Performance-Related Pay Committee

The members of the PRP Committee should be drawn from those levels of the organisation that will be affected by the scheme. Include at least one member from the personnel and accounts departments, and representatives of trade unions within the organisation if appropriate. The Committee will manage the design and implementation of the PRP scheme. Appoint a coordinator (someone with project management experience who commands respect and can get things done) to oversee the scheme.

2. Define the scope and coverage of the scheme

Will all staff be eligible for PRP or do you wish only middle to senior level managers to be covered by the scheme?

3. Gather information

Ascertain whether members of the Committee have been involved in this type of scheme before, and if so utilise their experience. The coordinator should carry out some background reading and try to find out how schemes in other, similar, organisations operate. Remember, however, that a scheme which works for one organisation may not work for another.

4. Draw up the scheme

The five most important points of a PRP scheme are that it should:

- be simple and easily understandable to all staff
- have a definable relationship between the results of the performance rating and the amount awarded

- be consistently applicable both among staff in the same department and throughout the organisation
- include an appeals procedure for employees not satisfied with their assessment
- contain a system of review and evaluation.

When drawing up the scheme the following areas must be included:

a) A method for defining performance measures

Two approaches are available:

- qualitative criteria for individual jobs (taking into account job specifications) or more general criteria to cover all jobs within an organisation (which can incorporate organisational goals, such as customer service, repeat business, and lack of complaints)
- quantifiable targets, usually financial but can include other measures such as increasing the number of service users or reducing the time for processing invoices.

The method used will depend on the jobs in question; a combination of both methods can be extremely effective. Ensure that there is a limit to the number of performance measures on which an employee can be assessed – generally no more than 10. Any number greater than this and rating will become complicated and time-consuming.

b) A scale for rating performance

Whichever method is used to define performance it is necessary to produce a scale to rate performance. Most rating systems use a six-point scale, for example:

Exceptional	Very good	Good
Satisfactory	Poor	Unacceptable

A numerical score should be assigned to each division of the rating scale (ie 6 = exceptional and 1 = unacceptable). These scales can be used to score each one of an individual's performance criteria or targets and then accumulated to produce an overall performance assessment.

c) A link between assessment and the pay award

The results of the performance assessment should be linked directly to an award of a percentage of the employee's salary (for example, a performance assessment of 3 is equal to 4% of salary). Payment of the award should be spread over the following year's salary. An award should not be made for anything less than good performance. Each employee should be informed in person of the award they have been given.

d) A timetable for assessment

As part of the PRP scheme each employee should have a meeting with their line manager at the beginning of the year to discuss and set targets, and agree on performance objectives. Regular reviews should take place throughout the year to identify and overcome any problems that may have arisen. Towards the end of the year a final meeting should be held to discuss performance and for the line manager to rate the employee.

An example of such a timetable might be:

Month 1	initial meeting and setting of targets/objectives
Months 3 and 6	performance reviews and identification of problems
Month 10 or 11	final appraisal and rating
Month 12	notification to the employee of any award due

The first and final interviews should be documented formally, highlighting objectives and targets, and one copy should be given to the employee and another kept on file. Do not discuss awards or ratings during the final meeting as it can turn it into a pay negotiation session. Remember these meetings do not replace an employee's usual development/performance meetings, which are often held on an informal basis.

e) An appeals procedure

It is very important that staff can seek redress if they feel they have been appraised improperly or unfairly. Inform each member of staff of the name of their first point of contact if such a situation occurs. This should not be the same person who appraised them. The organisation's personnel officer is generally the most suitable first contact.

5. Train staff involved in assessing performance

When training those managers involved in setting targets and conducting appraisal interviews:

- begin with the basics and go over the principles of PRP
- cover in detail the ins and outs of the organisation's PRP scheme
- coach them in negotiating employees to arrive at appropriate goals and objectives
- highlight how an effective appraisal interview should be carried out.

Hold practice performance interviews among the participants but do not attempt to cover everything in one session. Run refresher courses after the scheme has been implemented and remember to provide full training for new recruits.

6. Communicate the scheme to all staff

Use team briefings and individual discussions to convey the message and produce a documented guide to your organisation's PRP scheme. Include this guide in the employee handbook so that each new recruit will receive details as a matter of routine. Provide a contact name of a member of the PRP Committee to whom an employee can go if further information is required.

7. Pilot the scheme

Depending on the size of the organisation, it may be advisable to concentrate on one level of management or department initially. The experiences from this pilot can then be used to improve the PRP scheme and implement it on a wider scale. Always start the PRP scheme at the beginning of your organisation's financial year.

8. Review and evaluate the PRP scheme

The PRP Committee should meet at the end of each financial year to review the scheme. Obtain the views of both the employees and the assessors to identify any problem areas. Do some managers feel unsure about setting objectives or conducting performance appraisals? Look at the award figures; does it appear that some managers are being more lenient, or more strict than others? Are some managers featuring in the appeals procedure more than others? Take into account any changes in legislation regarding PRP. If modifications need to be made to the scheme, consult with the unions, then make the changes and inform all staff.

Most importantly, decide whether the PRP scheme is achieving its objective of improving employee performance. If the answer to this is no, then find out whether the scheme can be modified and improved or whether it should be replaced with an alternative reward scheme. If the answer is yes, don't rest on your laurels, keep reviewing and modifying if necessary, and consider the possibility of expanding the scheme to cover other levels of staff or departments.

Useful reading

Books

How to design and implement a results-oriented variable pay system, John G Belcher, New York: Amacom, 1996

Performance related pay, Alan Fowler, Winchester: Souther Provincial Employers' Organisation

Journal article

Making performance related pay work, Graeme Crombie, Topics ER Consultants, vol 60 no 1, Winter 1994, pp5–9

Dos and don'ts for setting up a performance-related pay scheme

Do

- Involve union officials.
- Communicate the advantages of PRP.
- Continually look for improvements.

Don't

- Make the scheme too complicated.
- Forget to train all staff.
- Hide the results of the scheme.

Implementing a Smoking Policy

This checklist provides guidance for those who wish to implement a smoking policy in their company or organisation. It is primarily aimed at those implementing a company-wide policy, although it is also relevant for single sites or departments.

Many organisations have restricted, either totally or partially, smoking at work due to pressure from employees and the requirements of the 1974 Health and Safety at Work Act, which places a responsibility on employers to protect the health of their workers, and the 1992 Code of Practice for the Management of Health and Safety at Work Act, which requires employers to implement methods to minimise the risks against health. The addictive nature of nicotine makes changing an employee's ability to smoke at work a sensitive issue, and it is important to help smokers adjust to restrictions by offering counselling on cutting down or stopping smoking. The aim of a smoking policy should not be to harass smokers, but should be to create an environment which is acceptable both to smokers and non-smokers.

MCI Standards

This checklist has relevance for the MCI Management Standards: Key Role A – Manage Activities.

Definition

A smoking policy provides guidelines for employees on where and when they can smoke in an organisation, states the disciplinary action to be taken against those who do not comply, and the disciplinary procedures to be used.

Advantages of a smoking policy

Through implementing a smoking policy, an organisation:

- creates a healthier and cleaner working environment
- complies with health and safety legislation on ensuring the health, safety and welfare of employees

- can protect itself against legal action brought by employees suffering from the effects of passive smoking
- shows a caring attitude towards the health of employees
- can reduce absenteeism through smoking-related illness.

Disadvantages of a smoking policy

A smoking policy:

- may make smokers feel they are being victimised
- may cause conflict between smokers and non-smokers (especially if smokers are allowed 'smoking breaks' in 'smoking rooms')
- requires careful and time-consuming consultation between the employer, employees and trade unions.

Action checklist

1. Designate a Smoking Policy Committee

The members of the Smoking Policy Committee should be drawn from all levels of the organisation and should include both smokers and non-smokers. The Committee will help manage the design, implementation and running of the smoking policy. Appoint a coordinator (not necessarily from senior management, but someone with project management experience who commands respect, has excellent communication and negotiation skills, and can get things done) to oversee the project. Include at least one representative from each trade union to which employees belong, to provide guidance on the union view.

2. Gather the views of employees

Workers' opinions on smoking in the organisation and the strength of feeling towards a smoking policy should be ascertained. (Undertaking an employee attitude survey is covered on page 93). These views must be taken into account when deciding what level of smoking policy will be implemented (a complete or partial ban). The survey will also provide information on the number of smokers and in which department or area they work, and shows employees that their opinions are important and valued on this delicate issue.

3. Communicate the need for a policy to all employees

Feed back the results of the survey to employees, showing how many people are in favour of a smoking restriction – including those who are smokers themselves.

Indicate the reasons why a smoking policy is needed including, where applicable, complaints from customers and non-smoking employees. Use notice boards, newsletters and team briefings to get this message across.

4. Draw up a smoking policy

Decide on the level of smoking restriction.

- **Total ban.** A total ban may seem to be the ideal, but it can cause problems with those who simply cannot cope without having an occasional smoke, leading them to sneak off and smoke in toilets and spare rooms. A total ban may be possible if it is brought in gradually, allowing smokers time to adjust to the policy by cutting down their intake or stopping smoking altogether.
- **Restricting smoking to certain rooms.** Providing 'smoking rooms' alleviates many of the problems of smoking at work, but requires that spare rooms are available, and that they can be properly ventilated and cleaned. Non-smokers may feel aggrieved if they see smokers disappearing to a smoking room for a 'break' whenever they like. If this method is used it must be properly supervised to avoid over-use/abuse.
- **Restricting smoking to certain areas.** This is less ideal than restricting smoking to certain rooms, as smoke can drift into non-smoking areas, even with ventilation. The Workplace (Health, Safety and Welfare) Regulations 1992 lay a duty on the employer to protect non-smokers from tobacco smoke in rest areas.

Make the policy site- or company-wide to avoid conflict between departments where smoking is allowed and those where it is not. The policy should also cover customers and visitors to the organisation. Where the visits will last a reasonable length of time it is advisable to offer a smoking room.

Draw up a list of disciplinary procedures for those who do not comply with the policy. Consult with union representatives over this. Designate who will be involved in any disciplinary proceedings.

5. Present the policy to senior management

The backing of senior management is essential to the success of the scheme, as they may have to deal with the grievances raised by the employees.

6. Prepare to help staff stop smoking

Every effort should be made to help employees who wish to stop smoking; this can be done by putting them in touch with local 'stop smoking' classes, or by hiring a counsellor who specialises in nicotine addiction.

7. Draw up an implementation timetable

Remember that there is a statutory time requirement regarding changing conditions of employment. Consult with union representatives over this. For many smokers, a restriction on smoking will have a major impact on their working life; they should be given time to adjust to the new policy, and so it can be helpful to lessen disciplinary action during the implementation period.

8. Communicate the policy to all staff

Ensure that staff are aware of the policy (a letter should be sent to all employees), when the policy will come into effect, and the disciplinary consequences of non-compliance. Make sure that areas or rooms where smoking is allowed or restricted are clearly communicated. Mention that the organisation has a smoking policy in any job advertisements.

9. Implement the policy

A member of the Smoking Policy Committee should be available at all times to deal with any problems that may arise. Signs and posters should be put up in areas where smoking is not allowed or is restricted. In organisations that frequently have visitors the signs should be visible as soon as an individual enters the building.

10. Evaluate the policy

Check the number of breaches of the policy and any complaints made by smokers and non-smokers. A breach of the rules should be acted on – a few breaches can lead to widespread non-observance. Remember that any evaluation procedure should be carried out regularly, at least once a year.

11. Make revisions/modifications

Use the information obtained from the evaluation to make any changes to the policy, for example, smoke may be drifting into non-smoking areas, requiring further restrictions or extra ventilation.

12. Feedback the results

Report back to senior management and all employees the success of the policy and any changes that have been made. Mention any comments made by suppliers, customers, visitors or health and safety officials with regard to the 'cleaner' environment.

Dos and don'ts for implementing a smoking policy

Do

- Obtain the opinions of employees on smoking in the organisation.
- Offer smokers counselling on how they can kick the habit.
- Stress that the introduction of the policy is for the benefit of all employees.
- Adhere to any disciplinary actions that have been written into the policy.

Don't

- Forget about involving the unions.
- Implement a policy all at once.
- Make exceptions in the policy – for senior management for example.

Useful reading

Books

No smoke without ire: how to plan and introduce a policy to control smoking in the workplace, Linda Seymour and Pat Leighton, Didcot: Management Books, 1995

A workplace smoking policy: how to plan and introduce a policy to control smoking in the workplace, Yvonne Bostock, London: Health Education Authority, 1994

Journal articles

Do we really need smoking policies at work? Hilary Maxfield, Journal of Employment Law and Practice, Vol 2 no 2, 1994, pp49–51

Breath of fresh air, Liz Hall, Personnel Today, 8 March 1994, pp35

Stubbing out passive smoking, Liz Batten, Personnel Management, Vol 24 no 8, August 1992, pp24–27

Do you mind if I smoke? Caren E I Naidoff, Management Review, September 1991, pp38–41

Useful addresses

Action on Smoking and Health (ASH), 109 Gloucester Place, London, WH1 4EJ, Tel: 0171 935 3519

QUIT, Victory House, 170 Tottenham Court Road, London, W1P 0HA, Tel: 0171 388 5775

Health Promotion Departments are listed in the local phone book. They are able to supply details of "Stop smoking" classes and also useful publicity material.

Thought starters

- Have you ever smoked? What helped you to stop?
- Have any of your previous workplaces employed a smoking policy? Did it work?
- What are the penalties for smoking?

Setting Up a Suggestion Scheme

This checklist provides guidance for those who wish to set up a suggestion scheme within their company or organisation.

Suggestion schemes have been used by organisations for a number of years as a way of gathering ideas from their employees to increase productivity, cut costs, or improve working conditions. A successful scheme has many positive effects on an organisation; most importantly, employees believe that management cares and listens to them. Implementing a successful suggestion scheme is not an easy process; careful planning, involving much staff time, is needed throughout. Suggestion schemes should not be seen as an alternative to regular communication and hands-on management, but rather as a means to supplement them.

MCI Standards

This checklist has relevance for the MCI Management Standards: Key Role A – Manage Activities.

Definition

A suggestion scheme is a planned procedure which enables an employee to make known an idea which will affect any aspect of work from cost savings and operational improvements to new product ideas and better customer service, and which may reward them for their initiative if the suggestion is implemented.

Advantages

Employee suggestion schemes:

- can lead to a reduction in costs and greater efficiency
- encourage employee involvement which improves morale and motivation
- help foster an environment in which creativity and innovation can flourish
- enable employees at 'ground level', who can often see problems and solutions that management does not, to be heard.

Disadvantages

They:

- can become a voice-box for the aggressive or verbose
- can provide a 'skewed' view if a few dominant characters over-use them
- need constant management to be effective.

Action checklist

1. Designate a Suggestion Scheme Committee

The members of the Suggestion Scheme Committee (SSC) should be drawn from all levels of the organisation. The SSC will help manage the scheme and provide input from its conception to its end. Appoint a coordinator (not necessarily from senior management, but someone with project management experience who commands respect and can get things done) to oversee the project.

2. Identify alternative schemes

Ascertain whether members of the SSC have been involved in this type of scheme before, and if so utilise their experience. The coordinator should, if possible, undertake a literature search to find similar case studies. Remember, however, that a suggestion scheme which works for one organisation may not work for another. A small organisation, for example, may not require a scheme at all, as ideas may be communicated to the relevant person easily enough anyway.

3. Draw up a scheme

After examples of suggestion schemes and the characteristics of the organisation are taken into account a scheme can be drawn up. Points to include when formulating the scheme are:

- Name of the scheme

The scheme should be given a name that will make it instantly recognisable to employees. Design a logo for the scheme that can be used for posters, leaflets and suggestion forms.

- Length of scheme

Running a scheme for set periods of time throughout the year has the advantage that publicity can be geared towards specific dates of start-up and so is more efficient. It can be difficult to advertise a continuous scheme effectively, keeping it fresh in the employee's mind. Suggestions do not, however, occur only at certain times of the year so, depending on availability of resources, it is advisable that a continuous scheme is implemented, with dates set for re-advertising, for example after Christmas shutdowns.

- **Format for suggestions**

The usual format for making a suggestion is on a specially designed form, which when complete is placed in a 'suggestion box' or addressed to an appropriate individual. Some organisations have successfully used verbal transmission of ideas from the originator to the co-ordinator.

- **Administration of the scheme**

The employees who will be involved in running the scheme should be identified. These will range from the person assigned to collecting and delivering the suggestion forms, to the SSC and to its co-ordinator. It is important to estimate the costs involved in administering the scheme, especially in the assessment process.

- **Assessing the suggestion**

The SSC should discuss individual suggestions and develop them where appropriate. Guidelines to be used when assessing a suggestion should be produced. These should include: originality of idea; ease of introducing the suggestion, and an estimate of the costs and benefits to the organisation. The assessment meetings should take place monthly so that feedback can be given to employees as soon as possible.

- **Rewards/awards**

Monetary rewards or gifts can be given to suggestors. The amount can be linked to any cost savings or improvements in efficiency, or it could be a standard gift for each successfully implemented suggestion. The Inland Revenue has rules on the amount that can be awarded to an employee which should be checked carefully.

The award can also be linked to the type of suggestion made:

- production – methods for reducing costs or increasing efficiency
- health and safety – ideas for improving health and safety in the workplace
- environmental – suggestions to make the organisation 'environmentally friendly'.

Consider providing an award that recognises the initiative of making a suggestion, whether it is implemented or not. Where a number of sites are involved, a 'Suggestion of the Year' award could be made which covers the whole organisation.

4. Present the scheme to senior management

A report detailing the proposed scheme and the advantages and disadvantages for the organisation should be made to senior management. Commitment from them is essential to the success of the scheme, as it will require resources to implement, rewards to find, and impartial control to administer.

5. Publicity

The scheme should be advertised at every opportunity so that all employees are made aware of it. The improvements made as a result of a successful suggestion should be communicated to the employees. Methods to use include:

- posters and leaflets on notice boards
- articles in staff newsletters and magazines (including details of 'winners' when there are any)
- inclusion as part of the induction training for new staff.

The initial publicity for the scheme should communicate the advantages for the employees and dispel any fears they may have.

6. Run a pilot

A small scale pilot scheme should be implemented. Any problems in administering it should be reviewed and modifications made.

7. Implement the scheme

The full scheme should be implemented. Any problems which occur in the running of the scheme should be noted by the co-ordinator.

8. Evaluate the scheme

At the end of a set period of time the scheme should be evaluated. Points to look out for include:

- the number of suggestions made
- the number of suggestions taken up and implemented
- financial savings made
- increases in efficiency
- costs incurred
- rewards/awards made
- types of suggestions made
- problems noted
- feedback from employees.

If the scheme is under-used, a thorough examination to determine why needs to be carried out.

After the SSC has discussed the evaluation of the scheme, any modifications necessary should be made. A report should be made to management detailing the performance of the scheme.

The evaluation process must be carried out each year throughout the life of the scheme so that improvements and modifications can be made regularly.

Dos and don'ts for setting up a practical suggestion scheme

Do

- Try to give feedback to the suggestor as soon as possible.
- Publicise the scheme constantly.
- Aim to get maximum participation.

Don't

- Implement a scheme without piloting it first.
- Forget to provide recognition of every suggestion (even if it can't be implemented).
- Under-communicate the advantages of the suggestion scheme to all employees.

Useful reading

Books

Ideas unlimited: how to run a successful suggestion scheme, James McConville and Andrew Wood, London: Industrial Society, 1994

Successful suggestion schemes, Gilles Desmons, London: Industrial Society, 1986

Journal articles

How to manage suggestion schemes, Alan Fowler, Personnel Management Plus, Vol 5 No 7, July 1994, pp28–29

Decent suggestions, Amanda Dunn, Human Resources UK, No 10, Summer 1993, pp16, 18, 20

Suggestion schemes: exploiting employees' ideas, Industrial Relations Review and Report, No 450, 24 October 1989, pp6–9

Useful addresses

United Kingdom Association of Suggestion Schemes, St Nicolas, Hoe Court, Lancing, West Sussex, BN15 0QX, Tel: 01903 755188

Industrial Society, 48 Bryanston Square, London, W1H 7LN, Tel: 0171 262 2401

Thought starters

- Have you ever wanted to make a suggestion that would improve efficiency? What did you do?
- What would attract you to make a suggestion to a suggestion scheme?
- What would prevent you from making a suggestion to a suggestion scheme?

Introducing a Whistleblowing Policy

This checklist is designed to help organisations to draw up a whistle-blowing policy.

In spite of the often ambivalent attitude held towards whistleblowers, there are practical reasons for treating whistleblowing as a policy issue:

- **wrongdoing will occur and there will be employees who will desire to stop it**
- **legislation protects employees who blow the whistle on activities that are against the public interest**
- **whistleblowing is on the increase**
- **retaliation against the whistleblower is neither desirable nor effective.**

A whistleblowing policy lets employees know what is, or is not, acceptable behaviour and allows sensitive issues to be dealt with internally, thus encouraging the employee to report wrongdoing while protecting the organisation from unexpected public disclosures. It is not a substitute for other management practices, such as performance appraisals and disciplinary and grievance procedures. Indeed, it is important that such interactions between manager and employee should be documented to enable the distinction to be made between proper and improper practice. The organisation should charge a senior manager with constructing and implementing the whistleblowing policy. This checklist is written to assist in that task.

MCI Standards

This checklist has relevance for the MCI Management Standards: Key Roles A, C and D – Manage Activities, Manage People and Manage Information.

Definition

Whistleblowing inside the workplace is the reporting, by employees or ex-employees, of wrongdoing such as fraud, malpractice, mismanagement, breach of health and safety law or any other illegal or unethical act, either on the part of management or by fellow employees.

Advantages of a good whistleblowing policy

- Challenges wrongdoing thus preventing its debilitating effect on an organisation and its reputation.
- Demonstrates that the organisation is determined to be fair and honest.
- Provides a mechanism for whistleblowers to voice their concerns without making them public.
- Saves the costs and bad publicity associated with public disclosure and legal action.
- Promotes accountability and deters bad practice.
- Improves the quality of customer care, particularly in service organisations.

Problems associated with a whistleblowing policy

- Whistleblowers may fear retaliation even though the policy strictly proscribes it.
- There will probably need to be a culture shift within the organisation.
- A code of conduct is needed to define the ethical context in which the organisation should operate.
- Employees may feel they are being spied on by co-workers.
- A policy will not work if it is simply a piece of paper which is filed away and neither communicated nor acted upon.
- Troublemakers may be encouraged to blow the whistle when there are no real issues at stake.

Action checklist

1. Create an ethical, open culture

Write, publish and communicate a code of conduct and ethics. Top management must make it clear that the organisation will not tolerate fraud and corruption and will deal with them seriously. The code should encourage employees who become aware of possible wrongdoings to report that information to designated parties inside the organisation, and assure them that their concerns will be treated seriously and that they will be protected. Apart from reinforcing an ethical environment, encourage an open and communicative culture where employees are not afraid to speak up. Provide guidelines, however, to assist staff in exercising their judgement, thus avoiding the reporting of all sorts of trivial matters.

2. Establish safe routes for communication of concerns

Appoint individuals or groups outside the normal chain of command to receive complaints of irregularities or other concerns. These people should have appropriate seniority and be well respected. They need diplomatic skills and should enjoy a reputation of honesty, impartiality and fairness. Make sure employees know who they are and how they can be contacted in confidence. Remind staff of other safe channels if they do not have the confidence to raise the issue internally, such as Public Concern at Work (see useful addresses) or an external auditor. These channels can also be used if the business is too small to accommodate impartial, confidential routes internally.

3. Protect the whistleblower

Make it clear you will support and not discriminate against concerned employees. Although they should identify themselves to the safe channel, otherwise give them anonymity where at all possible. The employee should be advised, however, that in many cases other people will know or guess who has raised the matter, in which case being open throughout may be more sensible. Protect them from reprisals by letting others know that harassment will be treated as a disciplinary matter.

4. Establish a fair and impartial investigative procedure

Make sure you respond to the concern by focusing on the problem, rather than denigrating the messenger. Take action to investigate and correct the problem or explain why management has chosen not to act if no action is warranted. Act quickly to reassure the whistleblower that action is being taken, to lessen the period of inevitable stress caused by the complaint, and to reduce the risk of retaliation against the employee.

5. Remind staff of their duty of confidentiality

The duty of fidelity is implied by the law in every contract of employment and prohibits employees from publicly disclosing employers' confidential information, unless it is in the public interest that information is disclosed. Remind staff that approaches for confidential advice to outside parties, such as lawyers, unions or other external safe channels is acceptable, but that the policy is designed to prevent any unnecessary public disclosure of concerns.

6. Safeguard against abuse of the policy

Make it clear that the malicious raising of unfounded allegations is a disciplinary offence. Protect managers from disgruntled poor performers by documenting performance reviews, disciplinary action and dismissal procedures. Remember, however, that some genuine concerns will be misconceived because an employee will never know all the facts.

7. Involve staff in developing the policy

To be effective there should be a sense of organisational ownership of a whistleblowing policy. Discuss the issues at the beginning, explaining the reasons behind the policy and dealing with objections and worries. Circulate the draft policy to employees or make it available for comments and suggestions. When the policy is complete make sure it is communicated to all staff and reinforced by permanent reminders such as attractive posters.

8. Review the policy

The project manager should:

- talk to any employees who have had reason to invoke the whistleblowing procedure
- find out if they were happy with the way their concerns were dealt with and if they experienced any harassment
- run an employee attitude survey (see the checklist on page 93) to find out if staff are comfortable with the nature of the corporate culture and if they think it supports the airing of concerns
- ensure that the policy is not being used in preference to other pre-existing, complementary policies
- remind staff of the policy annually.

Dos and don'ts of a whistleblowing policy

Do

- Communicate high ethical standards.
- Encourage an open culture.
- Appoint people outside the normal hierarchy as recipients of employee concerns.
- Document policies and practices to be used as support material when investigating whistleblowing cases.

Don't

- Use a whistleblowing policy as a sledgehammer to crack the nut of complaints and grievances that can be dealt with through normal procedures.
- Just publish a code of ethics – communicate it and reinforce it.
- Allow recriminations against whistleblowers.

Useful reading

Book

Protecting whistleblowers at work, Lucy Vickers, London: The Institute of Employment Rights, 1995

Journal articles

Blowing the whistle, Vivien Prime Tolleys Employment Law Line, Vol 3 no 10, April 1998, pp73–75
Whistleblowing at work: ingredients for an effective procedure, David Lewis, Human Resource Management Journal, Vol 7 no 4, Autumn 1997, pp5–11
Employee whistleblowing at Lewisham Social Services, IRS Employment Trends, No 590, August 1995, pp5–8
Whistleblowing: reaping the benefits, Marcia P Miceli and Janet P Near, Academy of Management Executive, Vol 8 no 3, August 1994, pp65–72

Useful addresses

Freedom to Care, c/o Dr Geoff Hunt, Chair, PO Box 125 West Molesey, Surrey KT8 1YE, Tel: 0181 224 1022. (This is a campaigning group.)
Public Concern at Work, Suite 306, 16 Baldwins Gardens, London EC1N 7RJ, Tel: 0171 404 6609. (This is a charity and legal advice centre.)

Thought starters

- If you encounter an ethical conflict at work how do you deal with it?
- Have you ever felt like blowing the whistle yourself?
- Is there a spirit of trust in your organisation?
- What procedures exist to prevent public disclosures of employee concerns?
- How can you discriminate between justified and invalid whistleblowing?

Undertaking an Employee Attitude Survey

This checklist provides guidance for those who wish to undertake an employee attitude survey within their organisation.

Employee attitude surveys are used by organisations as a way of monitoring the views of their employees as an occasional or routine exercise, or gauging the effect of a new policy, such as implementing a performance-related pay scheme. Surveys should not be carried out too often, perhaps no more frequently than every eighteen months. A very important aspect of any such survey is to report back the results to employees and act on them.

MCI Standards

This checklist has relevance for the MCI Management Standards: Key Roles C and D – Manage People and Manage Information.

Definition

An employee attitude survey is a planned procedure which enables an organisation to obtain the opinions of its employees on a particular issue or on the organisation itself, so as to take account of them in the planning process or make changes beneficial to the organisation and individuals alike.

Advantages of employee attitude surveys

Employee attitude surveys:

- provide data which can be used in problem-solving, planning and decision-making
- encourage employee involvement which improves morale and motivation
- allow management to hear employees' opinions of which they may not otherwise be aware
- provide an effective communication medium, or a sounding board.

Disadvantages of employee attitude surveys

They:

- require a good deal of time to carry out and evaluate
- incur significant costs in planning, implementing and evaluating
- can generate suspicion about the 'real' reasons behind the survey, and 'hidden agendas'.

Action checklist

1. Define the scope and coverage of the survey

Identify the subject on which employees' opinions are to be gathered. Be as precise as possible and be clear on how you will deal with views once they have been given. Bear in mind that a survey entitled, for example, 'Introducing teleworking' may give rise to all sorts of anxieties or expectations.

Decide who is to be included in the survey – all employees or one department or site, or one age group or one type of employee (such as full time permanent staff only).

2. Decide who is to run the survey

Appoint an agency to run the survey. This may be your own personnel department if you have one which is large enough, or a special working party drawn from all levels in the organisation. Consider contracting the work out to an external consultant if you feel you lack the necessary expertise internally; this will probably be more expensive but it may help to persuade staff of the impartiality of the process and that the results will be acted upon.

3. Select a survey method

Two principal survey methods are available.

- Questionnaire – to be filled in by the employee. Questionnaires are particularly useful when there is a large number of employees to survey and when the information is of the 'Yes/No' type.

- Face-to-face interviews with the employee. These can be on either an individual or group basis. As the contact is interactive, attitudes can be probed more deeply. The disadvantages are that interviews are time-consuming, are impractical for large numbers, can suffer from inconsistencies and produce results that are difficult to quantify.

The choice of method is dependent on the numbers to be surveyed, the type of information needed and the resources available.

4. Determine the questions and procedures

The questionnaire (or guidelines for interviewers in the case of face-to-face contact) should be formulated. Points to look for include:

- are the questions clear and unambiguous?
- will it take the employee a long time to complete?
- do the questions totally cover the subject?
- will the information obtained be easy to analyse?
- is confidentiality assured?

Ensure that the questions are not discriminatory in any way and take into account any likely problems with literacy or understanding terminology.

Devising questionnaires and holding interviews are not tasks for the enthusiastic amateur. It is worthwhile taking advice.

5. Pilot the survey

Select a number of employees and ask them to complete a questionnaire or undertake an interview. Ask them if they had any problems in completing the survey, and find out if they prefer to think about it at work or take it home. See whether the information obtained is what was being looked for. If necessary, make modifications to the questionnaire, or provide extra training for the interviewers.

6. Explain the exercise to all employees

It is crucial to ensure that the workforce understands the reasons behind the survey and the benefits it will have for them. This will alleviate any fears they may have and should result in a higher response rate. Depending on the nature of the survey, you may wish to explain to any employees not participating why it is being carried out.

7. Implement the survey

Distribute the questionnaires or arrange for the interviews to be held. To avoid loss of impetus, leave as short a time as possible for the survey to be completed (allowing sufficient time for those employees on annual leave). Ensure that help is available to deal with any possible problems. It is advisable to ask employees to return completed questionnaires to an outside agency to persuade staff of the confidentiality and impartiality with which their replies will be treated.

8. Collate and report results

It is essential to communicate the results of the survey both to senior management and employees if distrust and suspicion are to be avoided. In the case of employees it is usually advisable to provide only a summary as they may not wish to read a lengthy document. Make sure employees are told of promised plans of action resulting from the survey. Benchmark the results externally, particularly in the case of regular surveys which monitor trends. (Remember, however, that the survey may be so specific that a comparison is impossible). Survey analysis is a specialist task and you may therefore wish to contract this to an outside agency.

9. Evaluate the survey method

Evaluate the survey itself, for example the response rate and any difficulties which arose. Take these into account when planning and designing a follow-up or other surveys.

10. Follow-up survey method

It is often desirable to undertake a second survey once the plans of action have had time to take effect, to see whether the changes introduced have made improvements. In cases where little or no action is called for this is unnecessary.

Dos and don'ts for undertaking an employee attitude survey

Do

- Pilot the survey before full implementation.
- Report results of the survey and plans of action to all employees.
- Benchmark with employee surveys undertaken in other organisations if possible.

Don't

- Implement the survey without careful planning.
- Forget to note any problems in undertaking the survey so improvements can be made.
- Use the survey for a 'hidden agenda'.

Useful reading

Books

Employee surveys, London: Industrial Society, 1994

Building the responsive organisation: using employee surveys to manage change, Mike Walters, London: McGraw-Hill, 1994

Questionnaire design, interviewing and attitude measurement, 2nd ed,A N Oppenheim, London: Pinter, 1992

Journal articles

A piece of their mind, Hashi Syedain, Human Resources UK, No 16, January/February 1995, pp101–102, 104

Everything you wanted to know about employee surveys, Karen Paul and David Bracken Training and Development USA, Vol 49 no 1, January 1995, pp45–49

Surveying the scene, Mike Walters, Best Practice UK, September 1994, pp21–23

How to plan and use attitude surveys, Alan Fowler, Personnel Management Plus, Vol 4 no 6, June 1993, pp25–26

Thought starters

- Have you ever taken part in an employee attitude survey yourself?
- Did anything productive come from it?
- What would motivate you to complete an attitude questionnaire?
- What would put you off taking part in an attitude survey?

Setting Up a Grievance Procedure

This checklist provides guidance for those wishing to implement a grievance procedure within their company or organisation.

Employers have a duty under the 1978 Employment Protection (Consolidation) Act and the 1993 Trade Union Reform and Employment Rights Act to inform their employees of the person to whom they must take their grievance (usually their immediate line manager) and in what form they must present it.

Many grievances cannot be settled by a single meeting. A thorough grievance procedure goes further by providing a process, involving more than one level of management, which both the employer and employee can follow to reach an acceptable conclusion to the problem. Settling grievances quickly and fairly means they do not fester and grow.

MCI Standards

This checklist has relevance for the MCI Management Standards: Key Roles C and G – Manage People and Manage Projects.

Definition

A grievance procedure provides an employee with a hierarchical structure for presenting and settling a grievance at work. The procedure defines the type of grievance it covers, the individuals responsible at each stage, the presentation and documentation of a grievance, and the time limits by which the grievance must be presented and dealt with at each stage.

Advantages of setting up a grievance procedure

By implementing a grievance procedure, an organisation:

- complies with, and surpasses, the requirements of employment legislation
- can prevent a minor grievance becoming a major problem
- conveys a 'caring' attitude to its employees.

Disadvantages of setting up a grievance procedure

There are no real disadvantages to implementing a grievance procedure, but remember they:

- require time and resources to be effective
- can deter an employee from presenting a grievance if they are too formal.

Action checklist

1. Define the terms of reference

Decide which types of grievance the procedure will cover; often grievance procedures in such areas as sexual or racial harassment, job grading and collective disputes have their own process for settlement. Identify who the procedure is aimed at (for example, shop-floor workers only) and the levels of management that will be involved in settling the grievances.

2. Draw up the procedure

Consult with other members of the organisation, including trade union representatives, to devise a procedure. Try to obtain samples of procedures used in other organisations. Write the procedure in simple straightforward language so that it is easy to understand.

The procedure should contain the following:

- **Types of grievance**
  List the types of grievances the process covers. Refer other types of complaint to the appropriate procedures (eg sexual harassment).

- **The stages involved**
  Initially the aggrieved should be encouraged to have an informal meeting with their immediate superior to discuss the problem and see if they can work it out without using the formality of the procedure. If this does not work then the first stage of the procedure should be a formal meeting with the aggrieved and their immediate superior (give an alternative, such as the personnel manager, in case the supervisor is party to the complaint; however, the alternative should not be one of the higher levels of referral). By making the immediate supervisor the first point of contact, their level of authority is not undermined.

  The number of stages, where the employee progressively meets with higher levels of management, will depend on many factors, including the size of the organisation. There should be at least two stages to provide a minimum of one level of appeal, but too many stages can mean the process is lengthy and offputting. The name or preferably the job title of the person responsible for grievances at each level should be given.

The last stage should be referral to an external body such as an independent arbitrator or conciliator like the Advisory, Conciliation and Arbitration Service (ACAS), should it not be possible to settle the grievance internally.

- **Representation at meetings**
  A colleague or trade union representative should be allowed to accompany or represent the aggrieved at each meeting if they so wish. Specify at what stage the employee is entitled to representation – this can depend on the situation and the relationship between management and unions. The procedure represents the formal acceptance by management of the employee's representative as an equal partner in trying to settle the grievance.

- **Time limits**
  Realistic time limits should be set (in working days) for the presentation of the complaint and the management response at each stage. This time limit will get longer as the grievance moves up the hierarchy to more senior management, since the problem will be of a more serious nature and will require more time to deal with. A proviso could be included permitting the extension of time-limits by mutual agreement.

- **Presentation and documentation of a grievance**
  The initial presentation of a grievance need only be made verbally with the immediate supervisor. A written presentation might deter those who feel theirs is a minor grievance. Brief documentation should be kept of this meeting. For each stage thereafter, a record of information and events, including supporting arguments and evidence, should be kept to pass up through the stages for those not familiar with the grievance. The record should be agreed by the manager concerned and countersigned by the employee and/or their representative. This helps to ensure there are no misunderstandings when an agreement on resolving the problem has been reached.

- **Guidelines for the interviewer**
  The way in which the person responsible should prepare for and handle the grievance interview should be included.

- **Status quo clause**
  Arrange a status quo clause with the trade unions so that any industrial action will be deferred until a grievance has completed the full procedure.

3. Draw up an implementation timetable

In a large organisation it is often better to pilot the grievance procedure on one site or large department before full implementation.

4. Provide training for managers and supervisors

Conducting a grievance interview effectively is not easy. Training should be given to all managers and supervisors who may have to deal with a grievance. Ensure that they are aware of the limits of their and others' authority and that they understand the mechanics of the procedure, for example the number of working days in which they should have replied to a grievance and the documentation they should keep. Giving training to those responsible for holding interviews will help solve problems as close as possible to the point of their origin.

5. Communicate and implement the procedure

Ensure that staff are aware of the procedure (a letter should be sent to all employees along with a copy of the procedure), when the procedure will come into effect, and who the relevant managers are for each stage. Explain that the procedure has been introduced to benefit employees by providing them with a systematic way of airing grievances and reaching an amicable agreement in as short a time as possible. The same information should be given to new recruits; a copy should be attached to all noticeboards and included in the staff manual. Ensure staff have a contact who can answer any questions which may arise.

6. Evaluate the procedure

Regular evaluation of the procedure will contribute towards its improvement. The number of grievances and settlements, the subject matter of individual grievances and any levels of management that seem to have difficulties in handling grievances should be identified. Grievance records can help to analyse trends in causes of grievance. Employees who have used the procedure to settle a grievance should be questioned to ascertain any problems they may have had. It is essential to check that the procedure has been applied fairly and consistently in all cases.

7. Make changes/modifications

Alterations should be made to combat any of the problems highlighted in the evaluation. This may include offering extra training to certain managers or removing a stage in the procedure. Make sure the names or job titles of managers responsible for grievances at each stage are updated as necessary.

8. Feedback the results

Communicate the success of the procedure to all employees and let them know of any changes to be made.

Dos and don'ts for setting up a grievance procedure

Do

- Try to obtain copies of procedures used in other organisations.
- Define the types of grievance the procedure will cover.
- Train those who will be involved at each stage of the procedure.

Don't

- Make the initial stage too formal, as some grievances may not be aired.
- Set unrealistic time limits.
- Forget to allow the aggrieved an alternative to their line manager initially.

Useful reading

Books

Producing disciplinary and grievance procedures, Advisory, Conciliation and Arbitration Service, London: 1997

The skills of interviewing: a guide for managers and trainers, Leslie Rae, Aldershot: Gower, 1988

Settling disputes peacefully: procedure agreements, London: Institute of Directors Policy Unit, 1985

Grievance procedures, A W J Thomson and V V Murray, Farnborough: Saxon House, 1976

Journal articles

Grievance Procedures Bargaining Report, No 149, April 1995, pp7-11

How to handle employee grievances, Alan Fowler, Personnel Management Plus, Vol 5 no 10, October 1994, pp24–25

The complaint interview, Philip Morgan and H Kent Baker, Supervisory Management, June 1984, pp25–30

Useful addresses

Advisory, Conciliation and Arbitration Service (ACAS), Brandon House, 180 Borough High Street, London, SE1 1LW, Tel: 0171 210 3000

Institute of Management, Management House, Cottingham Road, Corby, Northants, NN17 1TT, Tel: 01536 204222

Thought starters

- Have you ever held a grievance at work? What did you do?
- Do you know how to handle a complaint from a member of staff?

Setting Up a Disciplinary Procedure

This checklist is aimed at those wishing to implement a disciplinary procedure within their company or organisation.

It is essential that an employer acts reasonably in dealing with misconduct and ill-discipline. A fair and thorough disciplinary procedure can help protect an employer against an unfair dismissal claim and the ensuing costs of a successful claim. Legislation aside, it is good personnel practice to deal with employee ill-discipline quickly and fairly, and to offer guidance on improving behaviour, so that problems do not fester and grow.

Although this checklist focuses on the mechanics of a disciplinary procedure, it is important to remember that good management, for example spotting problems before they become serious and identifying development needs to improve performance, can prevent many cases reaching this stage.

MCI Standards

This checklist has relevance for the MCI Management Standards: Key Roles C and G – Manage People and Manage Projects.

Definition

A **disciplinary procedure** provides employers with a structured approach for dealing with ill-discipline at work. The procedure defines the types of ill-discipline it covers, the presentation and documentation of warnings, representation at disciplinary interviews, time limits for investigation, and rights of appeal.

Benefits of disciplinary procedures

Disciplinary procedures:

- can help prevent a minor problem becoming a major one
- offer protection for the employer against claims of unfair dismissal
- standardise the consequences of ill-discipline throughout the organisation.

Points to remember about disciplinary procedures

There are no real disadvantages of implementing disciplinary procedures, but remember:

- they require time and resources to run effectively
- the objectives must be explained thoroughly to staff to avoid undue worry
- they are not to be used to replace informal warnings and performance monitoring systems.

Action checklist

1. Designate a Disciplinary Procedure Management Committee (DPMC)

The Committee should include, depending on the size of the organisation, at least one person from the personnel department, and from each level of management within the organisation, and a representative from each trade union to which employees belong. The Committee will manage the design, implementation and running of the disciplinary procedure. Appoint a coordinator (preferably the member from personnel, but certainly someone with project management experience who commands respect, has excellent communication and negotiation skills and can get things done) to oversee the project.

2. Define the terms of reference

Identify the employees covered by the procedure (for example, shop-floor workers only) and the managers who will be responsible for the disciplinary interviews. Define ill-discipline (both minor and serious misconduct), clarify legal obligations, and agree on the process which can lead to dismissal.

3. Draw up the procedure

Use the experiences, soundings and research of the DPMC to devise a procedure. Try to obtain samples of procedures used in other organisations and remember to write as simply as possible so that it is easy to understand.

The procedure should contain the following:

- Purpose
  An initial paragraph giving the reasons for having a procedure, highlighting the benefits to employees of a consistent set of rules and the importance of discipline in the workplace.

- **Types of misconduct**
  This should give staff an indication of the type of misconduct that would invoke the disciplinary procedure. Divide the offences in two – minor and serious. Provide examples of each:

Minor	Serious
Smoking (where appropriate)	Vandalism
Time-keeping	Fraud
Dress	Alcohol/Drugs

- **Warnings**
  Depending on the seriousness of the offence an employee will be faced with a series of warnings:

  Oral (confirmed in writing)
  Written
  Final written

  The ultimate penalty after this will be dismissal, although transfer and demotion may be considered.

  The warnings will be given to the employee after an interview, usually with the employee's line manager. Many procedures stipulate a length of time after which, if the employee does not re-offend, the warning is scrapped, but this can leave the door open to abuse of the system. For this reason it is best not to set a time limit, and to keep the warning on file. Remember that the disciplinary procedure should not be invoked unless informal warnings from the line manager have had no effect, or unless the offence is considered to be so important that instant disciplinary action must be taken. In cases of serious misconduct an employee may be suspended from work, on full pay, pending an investigation, then dismissed.

- **Representation at meetings**
  A colleague or trade union representative should be allowed to accompany or represent the employee at each warning interview. Consider stipulating that the union should be involved unless the employee specifically objects. On occasions when the offence also constitutes a criminal offence, a solicitor should be allowed to be present.

- **Investigations**
  All abuses of discipline must be investigated before a warning of any kind is issued. At the very least this involves hearing the employee's side of the story.

  Set a time limit within which to carry out an investigation into gross misconduct, such as deliberate malpractice. This should be not more than 10 days after the offence was committed.

- **Documentation**
  Detailed minutes should be taken at all interviews and kept along with copies of any investigation into the misconduct and any warnings issued. This documentation is not only useful for checking whether an employee's behaviour improves; it can also be used as evidence, in the event of an industrial tribunal, that correct procedures have been followed.

- **Plans of action**
  In the case of minor offences every effort must be made to help the employee overcome problems, thereby obviating the need to pursue the disciplinary process further. The procedure should make it clear that plans of action will be agreed between the employee and the line manager at each interview to enable improvements in discipline. A date will be given for an evaluation interview, at which, if progress has not been made, a more severe warning can be issued.

- **Appeals**
  Employees should be given the right to appeal against any warning they receive, as long as it is made in writing to their line manager within five working days of the issue of the warning.

4. Draw up an implementation timetable

In a large organisation it is often better to pilot the disciplinary procedure on one site or in a large department before full implementation.

5. Provide training for managers and supervisors

Training should be given to all managers and supervisors who may have to deal with disciplinary issues. Ensure that they understand the mechanics of the procedure and try to make sure that there is a consistency of approach. Give training not only in conducting a disciplinary interview effectively but also on general discipline and control; this will help solve as many problems as possible without the need for the full procedure.

6. Communicate the procedure to all employees

If you have disciplinary rules, by law they must be notified to employees. Ensure that staff are aware of the procedure (a letter should be sent to all employees along with a copy of the procedure), and know when the procedure will come into effect. Explain that the procedure has been introduced to benefit employees by providing a consistent way of dealing with ill-discipline. The same information should be given to new recruits and included in the staff manual.

7. Implement the procedure

Ensure a member of the DPMC is available to answer any questions that may arise, especially during the critical period following the communication of the procedure.

8. Evaluate the procedure

Regular evaluation of the procedure will contribute towards improving it. The number of times the procedure is used should be recorded, and any managers who seem to have difficulty in handling discipline should be identified. Employees who have been disciplined under the procedure should be asked for their views on it.

9. Make changes and give feedback on the results

Changes should be made in the light of the evaluation. These may include extra training for some managers, or re-writing some of the steps or phases. Communicate the changes made to employees.

Dos and don'ts for setting up a disciplinary procedure

Do

- Give examples of both minor and serious misconduct offences.
- Train those involved in carrying out disciplinary interviews.
- Document every action taken under the procedure.

Don't

- Take disciplinary action until the case has been investigated.
- 'Set the procedure in stone' – review it at regular periods.
- Allow the procedure to replace the need for good management.

Useful reading

Books

Croner's guide to managing discipline, Kingston upon Thames: Croner Publications, 1992

Discipline at work: the ACAS advisory handbook, London: ACAS, 1987

Journal articles

Discipline at work 2: the procedures, IRS Employment Review, No 592, September 1995, pp5–16 purple

Disciplinary procedures, Bargaining Report, No 144, November 1994, pp7–12

Examples of disciplinary procedures used in other organisations can be obtained from the Management Information Centre, Institute of Management.

Useful address

Advisory, Conciliation and Arbitration Service (ACAS), Brandon House, 180 Borough High Street, London SE1 1LW, Tel: 0171 210 3613

Thought starters

- Have you ever been disciplined at work? What happened?
- Do you know how to handle a disciplinary problem involving one of your staff?
- Are you up-to-date with the law on unfair dismissal?

Undertaking a Disciplinary Interview

This checklist provides guidance for managers who are required to hold a formal interview with an employee to correct a problem of ill-discipline, such as unacceptable behaviour or performance, as part of a disciplinary procedure.

MCI Standards

This checklist has relevance for the MCI Management Standards: Key Role C – Manage People

Definition

A disciplinary interview is a meeting between at least one manager and an employee (who may be accompanied by a colleague or trade union representative) to investigate and deal with an employee's misconduct in a fair and consistent manner.

Benefits of disciplinary interviews

Handled correctly a disciplinary interview:

- will tackle the cause of ill-discipline and provide solutions to remedy it
- can prevent further, more serious action needing to be taken against an employee
- will aid general morale, although an ineffective process will have the opposite effect.

Problems with disciplinary interviews

Ineffective handling of a disciplinary interview:

- leaves the employee unclear of the problem or how to improve
- can lead to claims of unfair dismissal if the employee is dismissed
- lowers the respect of the manager in the employee's eyes.

Action checklist

1. Prepare for the interview

Preparation and planning before the interview are essential in order to be fair and accurate in making a decision on the employee's conduct. The procedure – and the tone – should be as positive as possible, to help prevent recurrence and to improve behaviour where possible.

a) Gather all the facts
Obtain any written evidence, such as attendance records or production figures, which highlights the employee's misconduct. To obtain a balanced view, look for any special circumstances inside or outside work that may help to explain the problem – for example, low staffing levels or increased demand leading to work overload, or personal difficulties such as caring for a sick child.

b) Check the employee's record
Find out if the employee has already received one or more warnings under the disciplinary procedure.

c) Check the organisation's disciplinary procedure
Ascertain what options are available if the employee is guilty of misconduct, bearing in mind their disciplinary record and the seriousness of the offence.

d) Look for similar cases and outcomes
Confer with colleagues to see if they have dealt with similar cases and what the outcomes were. Also try to find out whether the employee is committing an offence which is widespread, for example persistent abuse of smoking rules or bad timekeeping. Is the employee being singled out unfairly over an offence which should be tackled organisation-wide?

e) Try to draw up a structure for the interview
Although no two disciplinary interviews will run exactly the same, a brief structure should be mapped out. Start by trying to define what you need to achieve from the interview and note important points that need to be covered. Thought should be given to the reasons, mitigating circumstances or excuses that the employee might make and how they should be recorded for checking out later. Consider who should be present at the interview, including witnesses.

2. Inform the employee

The employee should be informed in writing of:

- the reason why they face a disciplinary interview
- the time and place of the interview
- who will be present and who may accompany the employee at the interview.

Determine if all present should have access to all documents; in some cases this will not be in the employee's own interests.

Remember to give sufficient notice for the employee to prepare their case, and to make sure that the room to be used for the interview is available. This room must be spacious enough to accommodate those attending without congestion. A phone is useful to call witnesses to the interview but arrange for incoming calls to be diverted to avoid unnecessary interruptions.

The manager responsible for taking notes should be informed in advance, and witnesses called to arrange their availability. If witnesses cannot be present, obtain written statements from them.

3. Conduct the interview

Disciplinary interviews are stressful for both the manager and the employee. Their ultimate purpose is to create a satisfactory environment for all employees.

Remember to try to stay calm and collected; do not let the interview develop into a free-for-all shouting match, and ensure that the employee is aware that the interview is more than an informal reprimand.

The length of the interview is dependent on many factors, but it can become clear at any stage that the problem has either cleared up or that there needs to be further investigation, in which case the proceedings should be adjourned. Similarly, the interview should be called to a halt if matters get heated or unconstructive.

There is no set structure for a disciplinary interview; the following is one approach:

a) Introduction

- Introduce the people present and the reason for them being there (including a manager acting as a witness and taking notes, and any trade union representative).
- Communicate the reason for holding a disciplinary interview. Emphasise that it is part of the organisation's disciplinary procedure which exists to ensure that all employees are treated equally and fairly in these matters.
- Tell the employee how the interview will be structured; that is, with the case against them being presented first, followed by the employee's reply.

b) Present the case against the employee

- Detail the case against the employee, including any dates and times that breaches of discipline occurred. If the case has moved some way along the disciplinary procedure, present an outline of the previous stages, the actions taken and the results.

- Call on any witnesses to state what they have seen or heard, or knew; alternatively, read out the written statements if witnesses are unable to attend.

c) Allow the employee to reply

- Let the employee respond to the case against them, allowing them to present evidence, including witnesses and statements.
- Listen carefully to what the employee has to say, and do not interrupt them while they are speaking.

d) Discuss the case

Allow both sides to ask questions, particularly over ambiguous issues in the evidence. Ask open-ended questions to gain a general picture and more precise questions for specific information. It is important to ascertain whether there were any sound mitigating circumstances, of which you were unaware, for the employee's behaviour. Allow the employee to suggest ways in which the problem can be overcome.

e) Summarise the case

Following the discussion, the main points from both sides should be reiterated and the whole case summarised. When both sides have agreed this to be correct, the interview should be adjourned so that thought can be given to what action is to be taken or whether further investigation will take place. Try to do this as quickly as possible to keep anxiety or doubt to a minimum.

4. Inform the employee of the action to be taken

After you have made the decision (having conferred with colleagues), the employee and his/her representative should be brought together to be informed of the action to be taken, if any. If appropriate, actions for improving the situation should be agreed. Remember that these may involve the employer as well as the employee. They should be written down and signed by both parties and a date set for review. The employee should be informed of the appeals procedure if they disagree with the result of the interview or think they have been treated unfairly.

Dos and don'ts for undertaking a disciplinary interview

Do

- Gather all the facts before the interview.
- Leave enough time for both sides to prepare for the interview.
- Make the interview a discussion; let the employee have their say and listen to it.
- Record the evidence, the minutes of the interview and the outcomes.

Don't

- Neglect to check the organisation's disciplinary procedure.
- Assume guilt before the interview.
- Finish the interview without setting clear goals for the future.

Useful reading

BOOKS

Successful interviewing in a week, 2nd ed, Mo Shapiro, London: Hodder & Stoughton, 1998

The skills of interviewing: a guide for managers and trainers, Leslie Rae, Aldershot: Gower, 1988

JOURNAL ARTICLES

Help for discipline dodgers, Dave Day, Training and Development USA, Vol 47 no 5, May 1993, pp19–22

How to handle discipline interviews, Alan Fowler, PM Plus, Vol 1 no 5, November 1990, pp20–21

A discipline model for increasing performance, Robert N Lussier, Supervisory Management, August 1990, pp6–7

Useful addresses

Advisory, Conciliation and Arbitration Service (ACAS), Brandon House, 180 Borough High Street, London, SW1X 7AZ, Tel: 0171 210 3613

Thought starters

- Do you understand the workings of the organisation's disciplinary procedure?
- Have you ever had to discipline an employee before? How did it go?
- Have you ever been disciplined at work? Was it handled fairly?

Codes of Ethics

This checklist provides initial guidance for those introducing a new code of ethics or updating an existing one. It applies equally to the public, private and voluntary sectors.

There is a growing belief that organisations can succeed only if they are seen to observe high ethical standards. As a result, more are choosing to make a public commitment to ethical business by formulating and publishing a code of operating principles. The key difficulty they face in doing so is translating high sounding principles into practical guidelines, and thence into actual practice.

MCI Standards

This checklist has relevance for the MCI Occupational Standards: Key Role A – Manage Activities.

Definition

Codes of ethics are guidelines to the moral principles or values used by organisations to steer conduct, both for the organisation itself and its employees, in all their business activities, both internal and external.

Advantages of a code of ethics

A code of ethics:

- provides explicit guidance to managers and employees so they know what is expected of them in terms of ethical behaviour
- provides new employees with ethical guidance and a sense of common identity
- enhances the organisation's reputation and inspires public confidence
- signals to suppliers and customers the organisation's expectation of proper conduct
- promotes a culture of excellence by demonstrating the commitment of the organisation to ethical behaviour.

Disadvantages of a code of ethics

- Introducing a code can lead to cynicism if it is seen only as a paper exercise.
- Without proper guidance, different parts of the organisation may interpret the code differently, ultimately devaluing it.
- Introducing and implementing the code effectively will be demanding of senior management time.
- The code may raise public and employee expectations to a level that the organisation is unable to live up to.

Action checklist

1. Secure commitment of top management

Without the absolute and public commitment of top management, a code will not be taken seriously by employees. Commitment needs to be seen and felt.

2. Gain organisational agreement on the primary purpose of a code

Is the code mainly for the benefit of employees, or is it to be directed at those with a 'stake' in the organisation, including non executive directors, shareholders or even customers? Be clear on the major objectives sought and be aware of all the changes that such a code may imply – from a shift in the organisation's culture to the problems of whistle blowing.

3. Identify and define existing sources of values within the organisation

Consult existing codes, legal guidelines, policy memoranda and founding statements, and involve both managers and employees in their evaluation. Review the standard codes (eg those published by the Institute of Business Ethics or the Institute of Management), and those of organisations with similar operating policies to your own. Gain a consensus about the organisation's traditions and unwritten rules.

4. Prepare a draft code

This is best achieved through a small group, but drafting the code should be a dynamic process so don't exclude comments from employees at any level.

5. Include in the draft code:

- an introduction explaining its purpose, the need for it, and expectations about its use
- a clear definition of the organisation's mission and objectives

- guidance on handling relations with each of the organisation's constituencies: employees, shareholders, customers, suppliers, the outside community etc
- expectations about proper behaviour
- operating principles with realistic examples
- a formal mechanism to resolve employee questions.

6. Circulate the draft widely within the organisation and take comment seriously

Consultation should be wide and feedback and comments should be sought. This will have the additional benefit of reinforcing awareness of the code. If a significant amount of revision is necessary then a further circulation should follow.

7. Once the code is finalised, devise an implementation strategy

The implementation strategy must be both dynamic and continuous. Incorporate the code into induction, staff training and management development programmes. Bear in mind that implementation, like the preceding processes, may well benefit from a project management champion who can drive implementation forward with purpose, sensitivity and consideration.

8. Circulate the final code widely

The code should be sent to all employees. A letter from the head of the organisation explaining the purpose of the code and the expectations about its use should accompany it.

9. Establish a procedure for complaints, concerns and questions

Who is responsible for answering these? The line manager, human resource department or an ethics 'hot line'? Ensure appeal to a higher authority is built into the procedure.

10. Establish a mechanism to review the code's continuing relevance, and to monitor and evaluate its effectiveness

There is no set formula nor time-frame dictated by good practice. Nine months to a year may be appropriate for feedback, reaction and assessing any impact, again by further consultation perhaps on a one-to-one basis.

Dos and don'ts for effective codes of conduct

Do

- Make sure the code reflects the organisation's own values and traditions, and that it is in line with staff handbooks and operating manuals.

- Seek employee input at all stages, and encourage a climate which enables discussion of, and challenge to, the principles of the code without undermining it.
- Use plain language and avoid platitudes, jargon, legal and technical phrases or current buzz words when writing the code, and include realistic examples and factual situations to provide guidance.

Don't

- Use the code to impose new or inappropriate values on the organisation.
- Make the code too vague or prescriptive.
- Create an expectations gap between the principles of the code and the behaviour of the organisation in practice.
- Put ethical wallpaper on a decaying wall: it must be real, not a covering.

Useful reading

Books

Code of conduct and guide to professional management practice, Corby: Institute of Management, 1997

Ethical leadership, Stephen Connock and Ted Johns, London: Institute of Personnel and Development, 1995

Codes of business ethics: why companies should develop them and how, London: Institute of Business Ethics, 1993

The manager as a professional, Sheila M Evers, Corby: Institute of Management, 1993

An introduction to business ethics, G D Chrysiddes and J H Kaler, London: Chapman and Hall, 1993

Journal articles

12 steps to building a best practice ethics program, Frank Navran, Workforce, vol 76 no 9, Sep 1997, pp120–122

A global ethic in an age of globalization, Hans King, Business Ethics Quarterly, vol 7 no 3, 1997, pp17–32

Useful address

Institute of Business Ethics, 12 Palace Street, London SW1E 5JA, Tel: 0171 931 0495

Thought starters

- Do you really have the commitment of senior management or are they going to be distracted by other programmes and initiatives?
- Does the code prompt employees to ask themselves the following questions before acting:
  - Would I be willing to tell my family about this?
  - Would I mind if the press found out about it?

Developing a Mentoring Scheme

This checklist describes the steps and considerations involved in developing an organisational mentoring scheme.

MCI Standards

This checklist has relevance for the MCI Management Standards: Key Role C – Manage People.

Definition

Mentoring is a relationship in which one person (the mentor) – usually someone more experienced, often more senior in an organisation – helps another (the learner) to discover more about themselves, their potential and their capability. Mentoring should not be seen as an additional or supplementary management task, rather as part of a style and approach to management which puts the learner's development at the heart of the business process.

The relationship between mentor and learner can be informal – where the learner leans on the mentor for guidance, support, help and feedback. It can also be a more formal arrangement in organisations between two people who respect and trust each other and who have organisational backing to develop the relationship and positive outcomes from it. This checklist focuses on a more formal, organisational scheme.

Advantages of a formal scheme

Mentoring:

- shows organisational commitment to the individual's development in a non-dictatorial way
- provides an organisation-backed, uninvolved party who can guide, advise and listen in full confidentiality
- complements other forms of learning.

Disadvantages of an informal scheme

- Unstructured mentoring may be seen as patronage and giving unfair advantage.
- Ad hoc relationships may not take account of the way the organisation is developing.
- Informal schemes may well create gaps in organisational development.

Action checklist

1. Check the organisational culture

For a mentoring scheme to be successful, a suitable organisational culture needs to be in place. Check for:

- a clear and accepted vision of where the organisation is going
- encouragement of learning and development activities amongst staff
- levels of cooperation and help between different sections of the organisation
- a pervasive air of trust throughout.

The key to success is trust. It may be that a programme of change is needed before an organisation-wide mentoring scheme can be attempted with any hope of success.

2. Establish the goals of the scheme

Consider why you wish to establish a mentoring scheme. Common reasons include:

- improving and maintaining the skills and morale of staff
- providing an additional source of guidance and support to that offered by line management
- enabling staff to realise career development plans
- improving internal communication.

3. Get senior management commitment

A mentoring scheme which does not enjoy the visible support of senior management is almost certainly doomed to failure. Without this support, employees will feel that the scheme:

- is under-funded or under-resourced
- merely pays lip service to the idea of mentoring, with lack of authority behind it to progress development activities recommended.

Senior management commitment (or the lack of it) will spill down to mentors and learners and will influence strongly the time and energy that individuals devote to the scheme.

4. Find a champion

The mentoring scheme champion will preferably be a senior member of the organisation, possibly the person selected to manage the scheme. What is more important, though, is that they are seen to be actively supportive on a day-to-day basis. This will be demonstrated through their:

- help in developing the scheme
- willingness to become a mentor themselves
- involvement with others participating in the scheme
- commitment to training for those participating in the scheme.

5. Establish terms of reference

- **Clear up 'advice and advise' in a legal sense**
  Ownership of the mentoring process is with the individual learner. By adopting a joint agreement on a course of action, the mentor should not put themselves in a position of offering legal advice or guidance which could make them liable. Establish the difference between coaching, eliciting and agreeing action with pros and cons, and offering advice.

- **Confidentiality**
  All discussions between the mentor and learner should be strictly confidential. The only exception to this is if the learner agrees that their content can be relayed to a third party (for example the line manager).

- **Target audience**
  Establish who the scheme is aimed at.

6. Start small

Begin with a pilot. Nothing is foolproof or perfect; the scheme will need testing. If blunders of novelty are to be made, then it is best to confine them to a controllable sample. Do you have an identifiable cadre of responsible volunteers who are willing to devote their time, experience and energy to supporting and developing learners on a personal basis? Your pilot will need a core of such people to lend reliability, consistency and solidity to the process.

7. Identify and train the mentors

Mentoring should be a voluntary activity – a general invitation should therefore be issued to staff to attract those who wish to become mentors. It is imperative however, that a selection process is established to ensure a level of quality amongst those who mentor others.

Training (which may be offered in-house or by other organisations) is also important to mentors – they must be fully conversant with the mentoring scheme and what is or is not 'acceptable', and they must have a clear understanding of:

- the mentoring process
- the difference between mentoring and directing
- the boundaries of mentoring (for example psychological counselling goes beyond the boundaries)
- the skills necessary for effective mentoring.

8. Identify problems in advance

Work out what you are going to do when there is:

- conflict between the aims of the scheme and those of 'hidden' agendas
- breakdown between mentor and learner
- disruption to development patterns through new tasks or responsibilities
- obstruction by the line manager.

9. Work out the logistics

Make sure you have arrangements in place for:

- announcements, promotion and awareness
- questions, problems and reassurances
- the process of pairing mentor with learner
- proposing a framework for the first meeting.

10. Establish evaluation procedures

Plan to review the scheme on an annual basis against:

- the goals selected at the introduction of the scheme
- success or failure of mentoring relationships, identifying the reasons behind either.

Make sure you include learner feedback, as it is essential to amending or improving the scheme.

Dos and don'ts for developing a mentoring scheme

Do

- Provide clear guidance on what can, and cannot, be expected from a mentoring relationship.
- Run a pilot scheme first.

Don't

- Make too many assumptions from early success or failure – each learner will have different obstacles to overcome.
- Forget that all participants are volunteers – directiveness is not on the menu.

Useful reading

Successful mentoring in a week, Stephen Carter and Gareth Lewis, London: Hodder & Stoughton, 1994

An essential guide to mentoring, Stephen Carter, Corby: Institute of Management Foundation, 1994

Mentoring (Management Directions), Bob Norton and Jill Tivey, Corby: Institute of Management Foundation, 1995

Thought starters

- What management development schemes are in place in your organisation?
- What support is given to personal development planning or continuing professional development?

Investing in Your People

This checklist is an introductory guide to applying the Investors In People (IiP) Standard in your organisation.

MCI Standards

This checklist has relevance for the MCI Management Standards: Key Role C – Manage People.

Definition

The goal of IiP is to help organisations develop all their people to achieve business objectives.

Investors in People, a government initiative devised by the Employment Department (now the Department for Education and Employment), is a national standard aimed at helping organisations develop their staff. Resulting from lessons of best practice from organisations in the UK and abroad, IiP is based upon the premise that higher levels of skill and expertise benefit both the individual and the organisation.

Demonstration that the organisation is actively encouraging its employees to develop their skills to achieve business goals is achieved through assessment against the four principles of the national Standard which are described below.

Organisations obtain accreditation as an 'Investor in People' through a process of assessment carried out by the appropriate Training and Enterprise Council (TEC) in England or Wales, Local Enterprise Company (LEC) in Scotland, or Training and Employment Agency in Northern Ireland.

Advantages

Securing the IiP award will:

- demonstrate the organisation's commitment to training and development
- help the organisation in its recruitment and retention practices
- provide a framework for developing the organisation's skill base.

Requirements

There are four principal requirements for achieving the IiP Standard.

1. Public commitment from the top to develop all employees to achieve the organisation's business objectives

There must be a public commitment from the most senior level to develop people. This constitutes far more than a token signature or statement of intent. Commitment must be part of every senior manager's belief system. It needs to be written up in the Strategic Plan, supported by public notices of commitment and reinforced by regular meetings to encourage, support and reassure. The Commitment principle requires that everyone knows the broad aims of the organisation, understands the mission statement – if there is one – and understands that the organisation is committed to their development.

2. Regular reviews of the training and development needs of all employees

IiP requires that training and development needs are regularly reviewed against business objectives and also that a process exists for regularly reviewing the training and development needs of all employees (eg performance appraisal). The organisation should identify the responsibility for developing people (eg line manager or personnel department) and ensure that the resources required to meet the training and development needs are identified in the planning process and made available. The review process also needs to verify that managers are competent to carry out their responsibilities for developing people (eg through their own performance appraisal, by assessment against certain competency standards such as the MCI Standard listed above, or by attainment of a National Vocational Qualification). The review process will include – where possible – the targets and standards set for development actions.

3. Continuing action to train and develop individuals on recruitment and throughout their employment

IiP requires that all new employees are introduced to their workplace effectively and are given the training and development they need to do their job (eg there is an induction programme) and that the skills of existing employees are developed in line with business objectives. IiP requires that all employees are made aware of the development opportunities open to them such as:

- workplace experience
- peer group contacts
- work shadowing
- mentoring
- distance learning
- special projects
- private reading
- coaching
- delegation
- job rotation

- secondment
- a course
- attachment
- sitting-with-Nellie

Effective action should take place – and be seen to be taking place – to achieve the training and development objectives of individuals and the organisation. Managers have a responsibility to encourage and support their employees in identifying and meeting their job-related development needs.

4. Regular evaluation of the investment in training and development to assess achievement and improve its future effectiveness

IiP requires that the organisation evaluates how its development of people is contributing to business goals and targets and whether or not the development actions are effective. The outcomes of training and development should be evaluated at individual, team, and organisational level. The Standard also requires that top management continues its commitment to developing employees and has a clear understanding of the broad costs and benefits of developing people.

Evaluation of training and development activities is clearly difficult when the benefits of certain actions may not be realised until years later. To complete a post-training questionnaire would provide evidence but is often no more than mere tokenism. There are useful ways of evaluation, however, which can be built in to the process:

- at the performance appraisal where value can be recorded
- at team de-briefing sessions
- at de-briefing sessions with line manager or immediate superior.

In attaining these requirements the organisation will need to:

- compile a portfolio of evidence which should demonstrate that actions are being taken to meet the requirements
- send a letter of intent to the local TEC/LEC to register as an organisation undertaking IiP.

The organisation will also need to consider the requirements from the point of view of any major shifts of resources, any significant changes to the way people do things and securing staff involvement and commitment to the Standard.

Action checklist

1. Read the Standard

Try to gain an initial assessment of the implications for your organisation and the whole workforce.

2. Relate the Standard's requirements to your strategic thinking

Ensure that staff training and development are on the strategic agenda, as IiP requires.

3. Appoint a coordinator

Appoint a member of staff as IiP coordinator (this may be from the human resources department).

4. Conduct a training audit

Find out the difference between theory and practice – between what the organisation expects and what is actually happening – in terms of planning and evaluating development activities. Find out what staff really think about the four principal requirements of IiP. Diagnose the gaps between current practice and the Standard's requirements.

5. Produce an action plan for approval

You will find that some aspects of your practice are nearer to the IiP requirements than others. Most of the effort therefore needs to be put into closing these gaps. Much of the resource required will come in terms of time and effort – don't underestimate either.

6. Set up a steering group

Draw the participants from different sections of the organisation to help and encourage with implementation, monitor progress and channel feedback.

7. Make the commitment

This is a formal written commitment to your TEC or LEC to register, usually when you know that you have the staff behind you.

8. Communicate

Hold meetings to explain IiP, the commitment of the organisation, and what it means to departments and individuals. Get the action plan agreed with key people and communicate it to all staff.

9. Plan the training process

Establish a clear and distinct means of planning training and development and evaluating it (eg performance appraisals).

10. Assign and allocate resources

Especially management time, but also an appropriate commitment to a training budget.

11. Build up evidence

The assessor will want to examine written proof of commitment and action as well as visiting your premises to meet the staff. Start to construct a portfolio of evidence which demonstrates that the principles are being adhered to.

12. Check on progress

Build in a regular monitoring process to check that action is taking place as planned and that evidence is being recorded. This should not just be an annual event, but should take place two or three times a year.

13. Prepare a dummy run

Arrange with your IiP advisor for a pre-assessment exercise to learn how near you are to attaining the Standard, or how far away from it. This will help you to prepare for assessment.

14. The assessment

Assessment against the Standard is performed firstly against the portfolio of evidence submitted, and secondly by accredited assessors who come to visit the workplace and interview members of staff on various aspects of the four principles.

15. Post-assessment

Remember that being awarded IiP status is just the beginning; the organisation is periodically re-assessed to ensure that it still meets IiP requirements.

Useful reading

Investor in People toolkit: investing in people: the route, Sheffield: Department of Employment, 1991

Investors in people and management standards, London: Management Charter Initiative, 1993

Investors in people: your handbook, Frodsham: TQM International, 1993

For initial details (including a copy of the standard and an information pack) contact your local TEC/LEC

Thought starter

- Is staff development in your organisation haphazard or ad hoc? Or is it structured, flexible and meaningful?

ning Needs Analysis

heckist lays out the steps to follow to implement the process of Training Needs Analysis (TNA).

Effective training or development depends on knowing what results are required – for the individual, the department and the organisation as a whole. With limited budgets and the need for cost-effective solutions, all organisations need to feel secure that the resources invested in training are targeted at areas where training and development is needed and a positive return on the investment is guaranteed.

Analysing what the training needs are is a vital prerequisite for any effective training programme or event. Simply throwing training at individuals may miss the priority needs, and even cover areas that are not essential. Analysing training needs is not a task for specialists alone. Managers in today's organisations are responsible for all forms of people management, including the training and development of their team and its members. For this reason training needs analysis is a skilled process that every manager needs to know and be able to implement.

MCI Standards

This checklist has relevance for the MCI Management Standards: Key Role C – Manage People.

Definition

A training need has two components:

1. It is any shortcoming, gap or problem that prevents the individual or organisation achieving its objectives.
2. It can be overcome or reduced through training and/or development.

A training need can arise at three levels – the organisation, the activity and the individual. For our purposes an organisation can be seen not only as the whole company, but as any department, section or team with its own objectives.

At this level a training need is any behaviour or lack of skill that hinders the achievement of these corporate objectives; for example, it could be a lack of customer care skills that has a negative impact on the business, or a lack of interpersonal skills that affects staff retention.

At the activity level a training need applies to everyone doing the same work. So it could be that all tyre fitters in a company need to learn to use a new piece of equipment, while the members of the sales team do not.

At the individual level a training need occurs with an individual's lack of skills, knowledge or understanding. Or it could be the use (or absence) of certain behaviour that prevents an individual from being successful. For example, two receptionists sitting side by side do the same job. Receptionist A has a professional telephone manner while B is abrupt and offhand. B has a personal training need.

Advantages of training needs analysis

- Resources are targeted at identified priorities.
- TNA is a central plank in any effective development plan.
- Individuals and teams are helped to perform better, enhancing their levels of job satisfaction, morale and motivation.
- Having a TNA process in place enhances the organisation's progress towards Investors in People, as TNA is one of the key standards.
- It is a natural function of an appraisal system, where discussions take place on what skills need to be improved, and how.
- It provides a constructive base for improving performance.

Disadvantages of training needs analysis

There are no disadvantages to the process, but it does require:

- time and energy to plan the analysis systematically, and to analyse the results
- coordination of the results between different managers, to ensure that an organisational plan reflects the priorities across the whole company, allowing for economies of scale and avoiding duplication in different departments
- the full involvement of, and discussion with, potential trainees, rather than the subjective evaluation of their managers.

Ideally, it also means training managers in the process of TNA itself, to clarify what they are trying to achieve and what their approach should be.

Action checklist

Training needs can be sorted broadly into three types:

- those you can anticipate
- those that arise from monitoring
- reactions to unexpected problems.

1. Plan to integrate the identification of training needs

Training needs that exist in one department are likely to exist in others. It is pointless for individual managers to throw their own limited resources at each problem as it arises, duplicating efforts and dissipating energy.

Most organisations have a personnel function which organises training delivery. You may not be the person who coordinates the system, but you have an important role to play in collecting the best information you can on the training needs of the people who work for you and passing it up the line.

At the very least, liaise with other management colleagues to aggregate training need information, so that a range of appropriate training and development activities can be planned.

2. Anticipate problems or gaps in your own span of control

Anticipated needs often appear at the organisational or activity level. So a new machine coming into a workshop or office is almost certainly going to have training implications for everyone using it.

Alternatively, an organisation that decides to enhance its level of customer service as part of a corporate strategy knows that a programme of training and development is an essential contributor to its success.

3. Develop monitoring techniques

Some problems that fall into the category of training needs can go unnoticed while they creep up on the organisation. Active monitoring systems are essential to spot these.

Variance analysis is one approach to monitoring. This sounds technical but is a simple tool used by managers to monitor budgets. It translates neatly to the identification of training needs. When a budget is agreed, expected monthly expenditure is detailed. Any major variance from the forecast – upwards or downwards – triggers an investigation into why it happened and what the results will be.

In TNA, the budget numbers are replaced by performance standards and indicators which are as specific as possible. It could be, for instance, that even in a 'soft' issue like customer satisfaction, a standard can be set that says 95% of customers feel they received excellent service (the 5% allows for the small number who will always find something wrong, and those who always rate an experience as less than 100% on principle). Carrying out customer satisfaction surveys allows you to measure any deviation.

Asking questions in appraisal interviews is a form of survey, as the same basic issues are being addressed throughout the organisation. A fundamental purpose of appraisal is to identify individuals' training needs.

In addition to training needs that emerge as a result of an appraisal interview, a worthwhile approach to investigating one-off problems is to interview staff and customers. Regularly ask a random sample of people for their views on the same set of questions relating to general performance – for instance customer satisfaction levels.

4. Keep an open mind on unexpected problems

Monitoring will indicate where gaps and problems exist. However, it is possible to make the wrong assumption when faced with a particular set of circumstances. For instance, unusually rapid staff turnover in a small section may lead to a conclusion that the unsocial hours worked there are the issue. However, exit interviews with staff may indicate that turnover is a result of cramped working conditions and poor ventilation – something that training cannot resolve, even though the monitoring process has helped you identify the problem.

On the other hand, it could be that:

- the behaviour and approach of the section head are the root cause
- errors at recruitment stage mean that the wrong people are being taken on.

In either of these cases there is a training need – in the first case with the section head and in the second with those doing the recruiting. This could include you.

5. Identify the level

It could be that a training need is limited to an individual or an activity but it is more likely to impact on at least two, and perhaps all three levels.

If the organisation traditionally treats customers as a nuisance, it needs to change its overall approach. Giving one or two people training addresses the training need at the wrong level; organisation development is needed rather than individual training sessions.

6. Take appropriate action

If the training needs are within your own span of control, probably at individual or maybe at activity level, you can plan action to meet the needs.

If the needs appear to be at a wider level than the one you control, you need to make recommendations and proposals on a wider front.

Dos and don'ts for training needs analysis

Do

- Take TNA as seriously as you do the delivery of training.
- Make every effort to aggregate your findings with those of others.
- If necessary, work to persuade others of the benefits of collecting and collating data on training needs.
- Remember to consider potential needs at the three levels of organisation, activity and individual.
- Investigate problems carefully, so as to avoid making false assumptions.
- Include yourself as someone with potential training needs.

Don't

- Arrange any training without first establishing that there is a clear need for it.
- Simply send everyone on the same training event that you found useful and enjoyable – individuals have different backgrounds and experiences, so they have unique training priorities.
- Concentrate on obvious training needs at the expense of those you need to look for (for example with monitoring systems).

Useful reading

Training needs analysis handbook: a resource for identifying training needs, selecting training strategies and developing training plans, Sharon Bartram and Brenda Gibson, Aldershot: Gower, 1994

Identifying training needs: finding out what people need to know and why, David Reay, London: Kogan Page, 1994

Training needs analysis and evaluation, Frances Bee and Roland Bee, London: Institute of Personnel Management, 1994

Training needs analysis in the workplace, Robyn Peterson, London: Kogan Page, 1992

A guide to the identification of training needs, 2nd ed, T H Boydell, London: British Association for Commercial and Industrial Education, 1990

Thought starters

- How much of the training budget do you think was wasted last year – and why?
- What training do your people need that has not been arranged and is not likely? Why?
- Have you ever been sent on a course that you felt was irrelevant to your needs?
- Consider the motivational impact on your team of attending an engaging and worthwhile event.

Selecting a Video for Use in Training

This checklist provides guidance for those who wish to select a video to use in a training session.

Video is one of the most popular audio-visual media to be used in training. Selection of an appropriate video is not straightforward, as many factors must be considered. Mistakes made when selecting a video cost not only in terms of the price of the video if purchased (which can be up to £1000 for 20 minutes), but also through the trainees receiving inappropriate information.

MCI Standards

This checklist has relevance for the MCI Management Standards: Key Roles B and C – Manage Resources and Manage People.

Definition

Video is a medium used to store and display moving pictures and sound, and is viewed using a videocassette recorder and television screen. The use of the word 'video' in this checklist refers to those produced for a 'mass' audience rather than those that have been specifically commissioned by an organisation.

Advantages

- Very good at holding viewers' attention.
- Gives *'real-life'* information / scenarios that are not easy to create in a training session.
- All trainees can receive the same information at any place or time.
- Allows viewers access to *'experts'* at a fraction of the cost of a personal appearance.

Disadvantages

- Selection can be difficult.
- Can be expensive.

- Tend to go out of date, often quite quickly.
- Can be seen as just entertainment or as a break in the training session.

Action checklist

1. Define clearly the aims and objectives of the training session

The trainer should have a clear idea of how much s/he wishes the trainee to learn from the video and to what level.

2. Analyse the audience

The age of the trainees, their position within the organisation, and their existing knowledge and skills will affect the video selection. Videos with a strong comedy element may not be suitable for senior management, nor will a trainee gain much from viewing a video that examines a subject to a level much higher than they can understand.

3. Identify possible titles

Information can be obtained from supplier's catalogues, reviews in journals pertinent to the subject covered, or by word-of-mouth from colleagues or other employees. When drawing up a preliminary list of videos the following criteria should be checked:

- **Content:** is a subject covered in depth or just one part of a broader theme? Focus on the major objective of the training session and what you want to achieve.
- **Type:** the type of video should match the subject to be covered and the characteristics of the audience. Videos with a high comedy content, for example, may not be the correct choice for training on health and safety, but an overly serious approach may be equally inappropriate for holding people's attention.
- **Level:** the depth of treatment should match the level of understanding needed by the trainee.
- **Supplier:** dealing with a reputable and knowledgable supplier can help in the selection process.
- **Price:** when weighing up the price of a video its future use should be considered, since this will clearly affect its unit cost and hence its cost-effectiveness.
- **Hire/Buy:** in cases where the trainer knows the video will be used only once it is obviously cheaper to hire the video, if possible, from the supplier. If the video is for a course that is to be run a number of times then purchase becomes cost-effective.

- **Length:** although longer videos may seem more cost-efficient, this is not necessarily the case. The length of the training session dictates how much of it will be seen. Average attention spans vary from 15-25 minutes, so a long video may be impractical for one training session. In a short training session it can be distracting for the trainee to have to wait while a long video is wound forward to various 'highlights'.
- **Date:** check the date of publication (not all suppliers give a publication date) of the video so as not to include out-of-date material. Laws may be updated in the area of health and safety for example, and management thinking changes rapidly in some areas (industrial relations and the work-place, for example).
- **Extras:** many videos include facilitator's guides, overhead transparencies and handouts. These can be very useful as idea-stimulators or time-savers.

4. Preview the video

The most important step in the selection process is to view the video before purchasing it. This can be done at 'Preview Centres', of which there are many throughout the United Kingdom. Some suppliers offer their titles on a free loan for a number of days for preview purposes.

When viewing the video, ask yourself whether it:

- holds the attention of the viewer?
- uses language and terminology at a suitable level?
- meets the aims and objectives of the training course?
- matches the intended audience in the type of video?
- includes a summary or re-emphasises important points?
- seems believable to the audience?
- has no obvious distractions, such as old-fashioned clothing or poor actors?
- has an acceptable production quality?

5. Obtain the video

Hire or buy the video in plenty of time for the planned training session. Some videos are in heavy demand and bookings need to be made early.

6. Gather feedback from the trainees

This will aid in the evaluation of the effectiveness of the video and assist in future selection. Don't forget to ask about simple aspects like length.

Dos and don'ts for video selection

Do

- Clarify the aim of the course in your own mind.

- Try and view a couple of titles at your nearest Preview Centre.
- Listen to the trainees' opinions as to the usefulness of the video.

Don't

- Rely solely on supplier's catalogues.
- Make your decision solely on a recommendation from another trainer (their needs may have been different, even in the same subject).
- Presume one video is better than another because it costs more.

Useful reading

Books

A critical guide to management training media, William Ellet ed, Boston: Harvard Business School, 1997

Directory of Management Videos, Ray Irving ed, Corby: Institute of Management Foundation, 1996

Journal articles

Lessons for the discerning viewer, Terry Wilson, People Management, Vol 2 no 9, 2 May 1996, pp40–41

How to run a video based training session, Richard Roxburgh, Training Officer,Vol 30 no 9, November 1994, pp287–288

Good viewing: choosing training videos, Helen Swift, Human Resources UK, No 7, Autumn 1992, pp65–66

Choosing and using training videos, Sarah Rowe, Training and Management Development Methods, Vol 3 no 3, 1989, pp5.17–5.21

How to use video in training, Barry Smith, Journal of European Industrial Training, Vol 12 no 7, 1988, whole issue

A list of Preview Centres is available from the Institute of Management's Management Information Centre. Tel: 01536 207400.

Main suppliers

BBC for Business, Woodlands, 80 Wood Lane, London W12 0TT, Tel: 0181 516 2361 Fax: 0181 576 2867

Gower Publishing Ltd, Gower House, Croft Road, Aldershot, Hampshire GU11 3HR, Tel: 01252 331551 Fax: 01252 344405

Melrose Learning Resources Ltd, Dumbarton House, 68 Oxford Street, London W1N 0LH, Tel: 0171 627 8404 Fax: 0171 622 0421

Training Direct, Edinburgh Gate, Harlow, Essex CM20 2JE, Tel: 01279 623927 Fax: 01279 623795

Video Arts Ltd, Dumbarton House, 68 Oxford Street, London W1N 0LH, Tel: 0171 637 7288 Fax: 0171 580 8103

Thought starters

- Have any of your learning experiences included video?
- Which were the best training videos you have seen? Why?
- How do you use the information gained from video?

Evaluating Training

This checklist provides ideas and key points to build into your training programmes, to help you assess and evaluate the effectiveness of training. It should be read in conjunction with the Checklist on Training Needs Analysis on page 128.

Many organisations encounter problems with evaluation, largely because the evaluation process is restricted to the event itself, rather than being concerned with improvements in the performance of those who were trained.

Successful evaluation is a relatively long-term process which goes further than the immediate feedback on the quality of a specific event, even though that is important. Virtually all training events end with the participant completing a 'happy sheet' on which they record their feelings about the day or the course, answering questions such as:

- **how do you rate the tutor?**
- **were the handouts appropriate?**
- **were the physical surroundings suitable?**

This approach evaluates training input; it is essential for checking whether the training process was the most effective one available for delivering what was needed, and for improving future training inputs. But for the evaluation of training effectiveness – output – it is nowhere near adequate. Effective evaluation means checking that the long-term and permanent improvements or changes in performance, which you set out to achieve, have taken and are taking place.

Effective managers see the whole training function as a continuous cycle of identifying needs, delivering training to meet those needs and then evaluating what has been provided.

The problem is that the evaluation stage is the most difficult – not least because it is hard to pin down and quantify.

MCI Standards

This checklist has relevance for the MCI Management Standards: Key Role C – Manage People.

Definition

Evaluation is an analytical process of assessing the value of something. In the case of training, it focuses on whether the time and money spent on training have achieved the required results.

As organisations invest more in training and development, it is important to evaluate the outcomes of training activities in terms of:

a) achieving the goals that the training set out to achieve, and
b) cost-effectiveness.

Advantages of evaluating training

- Broadly, it can tell you whether what you have done has worked.
- It allows you to check that financial resources were targeted at identified priorities.
- If training has not achieved its objectives, the evaluation gives you information that should help you to improve it next time.
- The evaluation process confirms – or denies – that the improvements in individual performance which you sought have been achieved.
- The information gained feeds back into the appraisal process and helps managers discuss progress with individuals.
- Individuals and teams know what results are expected from training before they start, raising their commitment to, and involvement in, the training itself.
- Having an effective evaluation process in place enhances the organisation's progress towards Investors in People, as it is one of the key standards.
- It helps you to see clearly where you are in terms of development, and provides information about performance on which to base appropriate future training plans and processes.

Disadvantages of evaluating training

There are no disadvantages to the process, but it does require:

- commitment to training as an important and central business function rather than an optional or non-essential activity
- a disciplined and active planning approach rather than a reactive management style that concentrates on fire fighting
- precious management time to be spent on careful consideration of what is to be achieved and measured, and how to measure it, before allocating any training
- commitment of time and resources to the detailed analysis afterwards.

Action checklist

Remember the evaluation process starts as soon as you begin constructing a training plan.

1. Define what you want training to achieve

Having identified needs, quantify as specifically as possible what results and outcomes you expect. In many processes this can be relatively easy to define, for example:

- operate a machine safely
- use a graphics package
- set up a World Wide Web site
- construct widgets using new technology.

In many cases, these processes will be set to and measurable by occupational, organisational or national standards.

However, when it comes to continuous learning or changes in behaviour with no specific outcome, it is much harder to set measurable targets. Building up knowledge and experience in a specific area is fundamental to development but difficult to quantify. But you must do whatever is possible – for example describing behaviour that you want to see, or increased learning that you can demonstrate, or adding in a measure based on reduced numbers of complaints about late letters or returned telephone calls.

2. Turn targets into objectives

Objectives tell you what is to be achieved, by when. They should be SMART:

Specific – Measurable – Achievable – Realistic – Time limited

A training objective specifies what you realistically can expect the trainee to be able to do or to know as a result of the training.

If it is a skill that is to be achieved, the measurability aspect could be, for example, that within six weeks of the end of training, the trainee will be able to type a ten-page report with no more than six mistakes within an hour.

In the case of knowledge, avoid the word 'understand' because it is not measurable. Replace it with something like 'state', 'explain' or 'describe', because they are checkable and the trainee will need to have absorbed the knowledge in order to meet the objective.

3. Make sure everyone knows the objectives from the start

This includes:

- the trainees, in the information they receive in advance – both via personal briefings from their manager and from any published materials they get as joining instructions
- their managers (if you are arranging the training on behalf of other departments), so they know what their staff should be able to do as a result of the training
- the trainers – this may sound obvious, but they need to design the training based on what it should achieve, rather than the areas in which they can train others (which may be different).

4. Design methods for comparing results with objectives

The best way to do this is to get people together to come up with one agreed and consistent approach. It may involve forms, questionnaires, observation checklists, feedback meetings or statistical data, but the key point is that you must design the assessment procedures early on.

Immediate feedback is important, but do assess performance improvements over a realistic time span, often weeks and sometimes months. This allows time for the training to be applied and practised, leading to the actual outcomes you want to evaluate.

5. Evaluate the input

It is here that the 'happy sheets' are useful, to get a picture of the effectiveness of the actual training experience. Often, small and apparently insignificant points in the training environment – a noisy or stuffy room, tatty handouts or no coffee breaks – will have a massively disproportionate impact on the effectiveness of the event itself.

In the wider picture of objectives, having identified what you are going to measure, and when and how, the actual process of evaluation is a matter of comparing results with expectations.

6. Use the results

The information gained from evaluation is critical in starting the training cycle again, and planning what needs to be tackled next year, and how. Learning from experience, evaluation sets out key facts and measures of progress more clearly than any sort of gut reaction or guesswork.

Dos and don'ts for evaluating training

Do

- Specify the outcomes and results required, as objectives.
- Design the assessment and evaluation procedures early on.
- Involve other managers with a stake in the training outcomes.
- Review with an open mind what the evaluation tells you – mistakes and failures can be more helpful in making continuous improvements than convincing yourself it really was all right, when it wasn't.

Don't

- Avoid setting measures for the hardest-to-measure activities; if the best available is rough and ready, it remains the best available and it is much better than doing nothing.
- Try to justify poor results with excuses – if there is a lesson to be learned, value it.
- Concentrate only on the immediate feedback via 'happy sheets' or the longer-term outcomes of training – evaluate both.
- Give up – evaluating training is widely regarded as the most difficult aspect of the training function.

Useful reading

Training evaluation: managing best practice, London: Industrial Society, 1994

Evaluating training, David G Reay, London: Kogan Page, 1994

Handbook of training evaluation and measurement methods, 2nd ed, Jack J Phillips, London: Kogan Page, 1991

Evaluating training effectiveness: translating theory into practice, Peter Bramley, London: McGraw Hill, 1990

Thought starters

- How do you find out now whether training is achieving the right results?
- Wouldn't you like to know which training activities were effective and which could be improved?
- Aren't there some training activities that you already believe either don't work or could be improved, but you haven't got any evidence on which to base a case for improvement?

Planning a Workshop

This checklist describes how to plan and run a workshop.

MCI Standards

This checklist has relevance for the MCI Management Standards: Key Role D – Manage Information.

Definition

Workshops are not just meetings, nor lectures, nor seminars, nor discussions, but may well contain various elements of all, or some, of these. They are principally gatherings of anything from four to over ten people called together in an informal environment, conducive to creativity, in order to tackle a problem or achieve an objective. Workshops are appropriate for the study of broader issues, ones that deserve deeper analysis than can be achieved in ordinary meetings, or ones that require brainstorming or imaginative thinking.

Workshops do not have a 'chair', or a leader as such, but a facilitator who creates an open, relaxed atmosphere to encourage contributions from the participants.

A workshop can therefore be a group event or learning occasion or training session at which participants are the major contributors, or learn from each other or where the experience of the participants is more important than the knowledge of the workshop facilitator.

Advantages of workshops

Workshops are good for:

- securing group ownership of the objective
- getting maximum contributions from people
- involving people as fully as possible
- brainstorming ideas
- coming up with the right questions and constructive alternatives
- formulating a rough plan of action.

Disadvantages

Workshops are inappropriate if:

- you need to collate or analyse complex or detailed information
- you need to investigate mistakes or failure
- you need to make a final decision.

They do not work when:

- some individuals dominate
- people do not want to be there.

Action checklist

1. Select a facilitator

Determine whether the facilitator should be internal or external. Internal staff can be used if:

- the issue is not too complex
- the issue is not really contentious
- the staff member has some experience as a facilitator.

An external facilitator should be used when the above factors do not apply.

The facilitator should feel comfortable with running activity-based sessions and should be able to:

- indicate to participants what expected outcomes or targets are
- have clear plans and tactics on how to get there
- do as much as possible to ensure that participants own what they have achieved at the end.

2. Clarify what must be achieved

Identify the objectives of the workshop, deadlines to meet, and any opposing ideologies to reconcile. Ensure objectives are measurable.

3. Identify participants

Participants must be able to make a worthwhile contribution. Pay attention to the best mix of people and to any potential conflicts which will need to be managed.

4. Select a venue

This must have appropriate facilities – equipment, room-size and atmosphere are an easy oversight. Give some thought to a flexible workshop structure with content or themes for an outline programme, paying attention to syndicate rooms for group-working. Where it is important to 'step aside' and think afresh, a venue outside the premises should be considered – this frees the minds of participants as they will not be constantly thinking of work waiting for them a few yards away.

5. Obtain equipment

Think of all the fiddly bits and pieces that may seem trivial but can be enormously helpful when a session is in full swing ie glue, scissors, Blu-Tack, OHP, flipchart and pens that work, paper-clips or stapler etc. Get the room layout to suit your needs. Seating patterns can make a difference to discussion.

6. Establish groundrules

This is particularly important with brainstorming sessions, and with groups of mixed seniority but keep rules limited: the more rules, the more inhibiting it may become.

7. Assess what the participants need to know in advance

Perhaps set a pre-workshop task, but keep pre-workshop information to a minimum as the focus is on group activity. Be aware of preconceived ideas and fears, and prepare in advance how to dispose of them.

8. Work out a time-table

Workshops can last from half a day to two or three days, depending on the topic(s). Design the day(s) flexibly allowing for comfortable proportions of plenary to group-working sessions. Take into account the concentration required of the participants. Try to work a balanced mix between active and passive sessions. Remember to remain in control but be flexible when events by-pass or over-rule your scheduling.

Allow adequate time for coffee/tea breaks – participants need time to absorb ideas and chat with one another. If the workshop lasts more than one day, it is often useful to start the first day with lunch so that people can relax and get to know one another.

9. Plan how the workshop will begin

An immediate – but appropriate – ice-breaker can help establish the atmosphere you wish to create and can also help with introductions. After the ice-breaker, set the scene, clarify why you all there, and explain the process so that all are comfortable with it.

10. Make the workshop enjoyable

Everyone will get more from the workshop if it is an enjoyable experience.

Dos and don'ts for workshops

Do

- Foster informality.
- Focus on getting the group to work collectively.
- Adopt tasks and activities which are meaningful for the participants.
- Allow and encourage participants to solve their own problems.
- Get the group to own their findings and recommendations.
- Finish with a summary of what has been agreed or achieved.
- Allocate responsibilities and arrange for a follow-up.

Don't

- Allow things to become too relaxed.
- Worry about an individual's non-participation at the expense of overall group success.
- Spoon-feed.
- Seek to dominate thinking or try to impress with your knowledge.
- Spend much time lecturing or presenting.
- Indulge too many red-herrings.

Measuring workshop output

Measuring the success or failure of a workshop goes beyond mere participant satisfaction of – hopefully – an enjoyable and constructive session, or sessions. It is measured in terms of:

- to what extent measurable objectives were progressed, advanced or achieved
- what thinking, behaviour or activity changes have taken place, will take place or have been confirmed as a result of the workshop
- what action results as a consequence of the workshop.

Useful reading

Books

Workshops that work: 100 ideas to make your training events more effective, Tom Bourner, Vivien Marting and Phil Race, London: McGraw Hill, 1993

Icebreakers, Ken Jones, London: Kogan Page, 1991

Journal articles

How to make a workshop work, J Hargreaves, Industrial Marketing Digest, vol 13 no 4, 1988, pp 57–60

Improving working relationships: group effectiveness training, Brian Lusher, Journal of European Industrial Training, vol 14 no 5, 1990, pp 4–20

Experiential workshops for managers, Bill Peters, Training Officer, vol 27 no 6, 1991, pp 179–181

A case for workshops, Mark Langley, Training Officer, vol 24 no 4, 1988, pp 116–120

Thought starters

Are there more than daily routine:

- questions to clarify
- alternatives to construct
- tactics to determine
- proposals to clarify
- initial decisions to test and agree
- techniques to assimilate
- skills to practise

and people with appropriate experience who can help to achieve the required outcome?

Planning Assessment and Development Centres

This checklist is for managers who are considering the use of assessment or development centres in their organisation. Although assessment centres have been traditionally used for selection and recruitment, companies are increasingly examining their potential role in training and development, for the assessment of competence associated with National Vocational Qualifications (NVQ/SVQs), and even as an aid to support potential candidates for redundancy.

The typical exercises employed in such centres include leaderless group discussions, formal exercises with rotating leaders, business games, role-play, fact-finding exercises, presentations, structured interviews, in-tray exercises, paper-based tests and psychometric tests.

MCI Standards

This checklist has relevance for the MCI Management Standards: Key Roles B and C – Manage Resources and Manage People.

Definition

An assessment centre consists of a carefully designed programme of job related simulation exercises, in which the performance of a group of participants is observed and evaluated by specially trained assessors, who evaluate each participant against predetermined criteria.

Development centres are similar in design and structure, but have a very different purpose. Because they are designed to help participants learn more about themselves, development centres generally provide much more feedback from assessors.

Advantages of assessment and development centres

Assessment and development centres:

- have a high level of reliability in predicting future job performance (three times as high as interviews)
- provide a clear structure and logic, acceptable to participants and easily evaluated
- offer a reliable and objective way of assessing people against a diverse set of criteria
- present a prestigious image of the company
- provide insight into the nature of jobs and the culture of the organisation
- make it easier to present negative feedback to participants
- prevent poorly qualified candidates from being overlooked
- support the company's strategic processes for human resource management.

Disadvantages of assessment and development centres

They:

- are expensive and demanding to develop and maintain
- require a high level of expertise
- necessitate regular training and updating.

Action checklist

1. Define the objectives

Clarify the reasons for introducing a centre and ensure that the necessary resources are available. Try to justify the costs on the basis of predicted improvements in selection success and the current cost of poor selection. Once you have done this, you will need to sell the concept to the rest of the organisation. Don't forget to develop some form of policy statement to provide guidance on future plans.

2. Carry out job analyses

Effective job analysis is the key to success with assessment and development centres. If the behaviours and the criteria used by assessors are general and unrelated to specific jobs, the probability of success will be reduced.

The special tools that can be used to analyse job roles include:

- direct observation and work study
- structured interviews

- critical incident analysis
- repertory grid analysis
- job analysis questionnaires.

3. Design the centre

Designing a successful centre is really an art form as well as a science. Designers need to take into account the following factors:

- the relevance of exercises to the job
- the participants' backgrounds
- the relative importance of criteria (weighting)
- an interesting and balanced mix of exercises
- time and resource constraints.

Experienced designers like to create a matrix or grid of possible exercises mapped against the criteria. After selecting suitable items, they create a script for the centre, so that the participants are presented with a coherent picture for the whole experience (for example, the centre might be focused on a key issue or business simulation). The key stages in designing assessment and development centres are to:

- establish a design team
- produce the first draft
- try out the exercises
- review and edit the exercises
- develop guidelines for assessors.

4. Implement assessor training

No matter how well a centre has been designed, its effectiveness will ultimately depend on the quality of assessment. Assessors must be carefully selected and prepared. Assessors need to be familiar with the requirements of the job and are therefore often line managers. Key issues for the organisation are:

- Who should be assessors? How do we find assessors for more senior posts?
- How many assessors do we need? How many participants will there be? How often will centres be held?
- What qualities are we looking for in assessors? For example, committed, good observers, analytical, attention to detail, respected, counselling experience, etc.
- What are the training objectives? For example, thorough knowledge of techniques, standards, ability to record behaviour, feedback, objectivity, etc.
- What should the content of the training sessions be?

5. Plan and administer the centre

Assessment and development centres require meticulous planning so that in theory at least they will run automatically on the day. Issues that need to be considered by the team include:

- the variety and number of people to be brought together, such as an administrator, assessors, role players, resource providers
- the schedule for exercises – for example, start with a group exercise, ensure variety, include flexibility in timings, allow for altering schedules
- the master schedule or plan showing the time and location of all exercises and individuals
- room and equipment allocations
- briefing procedures – for example, joining instructions, expectations and arrangements for briefing assessors and participants
- checklists for all concerned.

6. Run the centre

It is important to select an able administrator to run the centre, who can deal with every eventuality smoothly. A typical programme might go as follows:

- Start the centre – check facilities, label rooms, finalise/adjust timetables, prepare rooms, provide photos of participants, brief assessors, and check paperwork.
- Brief participants – on the nature of the exercises, the roles of assessors, expectations and feedback arrangements.
- Administer exercises with suitable opportunities for review of progress.
- Provide a closing session to participants – hand out evaluation forms, explain feedback and follow-up arrangements, and say thank-yous.
- Hold the assessor 'wash-up' session – ensure completion of all work, review and reach agreement on overall ratings, document results, resolve disagreements in ratings, and allocate final responsibilities.

7. Report back

The centre's report should reflect the main purpose of the centre and would normally contain:

- a summary of the individual performance, probably with recommendations
- a summary evaluation for each criterion, including ratings and justification
- development needs and action plans.

8. Evaluate and modify centres

Assessment and development centres should continually evolve if they are to serve the organisation well. Every centre should contain rigorous procedures for quality assurance and there should be regular reviews of the design. Jobs change and there are always new ways available of assessing criteria.

Dos and don'ts for planning assessment and development centres

Do

- Question the design at regular intervals.
- Involve key stakeholders in the process.
- Plan meticulously.
- Brief the participants carefully.
- Ensure that participants are provided with clear feedback on their performance.
- Assume that everything will go wrong on the day – plan for all contingencies.

Don't

- Consider assessment centres unless you are prepared to run them properly.
- Allow cost to put you off – assessment and development centres may be cheaper when compared directly with the hidden costs of traditional methods.
- Assume that good managers automatically make good assessors.

Useful reading

Assessment and development centres, Iain Ballantyne and Nigel Povah, Aldershot: Gower, 1995

Development centres: realising the potential of your employees through assessment and development, Geoff Lee and David Beard, Maidenhead: McGraw Hill, 1994

Assessment centres: identifying and developing competence, 2nd ed, Charles Woodruffe, London: Institute of Personnel Management, 1993

Assessment centres, IDS Study, no 569, Jan 1995

Thought starters

- Have you ever added up the cost of unsuccessful recruitment?
- Have you ever considered direct assessment as a way of identifying training needs accurately? Or do you leave it to people to suggest training?
- Have you ever considered the possibility of using assessment or development centres to identify future career paths for those faced with possible redundancy? Can you always afford to lose those who rush to take up voluntary redundancy?

Further *Business Checklists* titles from Hodder & Stoughton and the Institute of Management all at £8.99

0 340 74292 5	Information & Financial Management	❐
0 340 74290 9	Marketing & Strategy	❐
0 340 74291 7	Operations & Quality Management	❐
0 340 74288 7	People Management	❐
0 340 74294 1	Personal Effectiveness & Career Development	❐
0 340 74293 3	Small Business Management	❐

All Hodder & Stoughton books are available from your local bookshop or can be ordered direct from the publisher. Just tick the titles you want and fill in the form below. Prices and availability subject to change without notice.

To: Hodder & Stoughton Ltd, Cash Sales Department, Bookpoint, 78 Milton Park, Abingdon, Oxon OX14 4TD. If you have a credit card you may order by telephone – 01235 400414
fax – 01235 400454
E-mail address: orders@bookpoint.co.uk

Please enclose a cheque or postal order made payable to Bookpoint Ltd to the value of the cover price and allow the following for postage and packaging:

UK & BFPO: £4.30 for one book; £6.30 for two books; £8.30 for three books.

OVERSEAS & EIRE: £4.80 for one book; £7.10 for 2 or 3 books (surface mail).

Name: ....

Address: ....

....

....

If you would prefer to pay by credit card, please complete:

Please debit my Visa/Mastercard/Diner's Card/American Express (delete as appropriate) card no:

❐ ❐ ❐ ❐ ❐ ❐ ❐ ❐ ❐ ❐ ❐ ❐ ❐ ❐ ❐ ❐

Signature .... Expiry date ....